Discovering Why God
Wants Us to Care for Each Other.

COMMUNITY

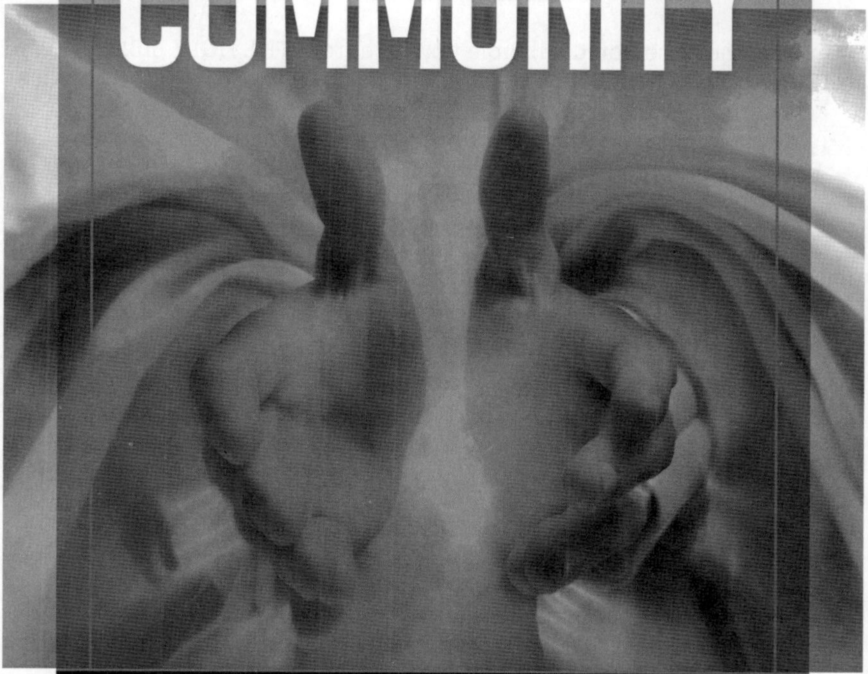

TROY FITZGERALD

Nampa, Idaho | www.pacificpress.com

Cover design by Gerald Lee Monks
Cover design resources from iStockphoto.com | joshblake
Inside design by Lauren Heinrich, Jessica Coffee

Purchase additional copies of this book by calling toll-free 1-800-765-6955 or by visiting http://www.adventistbookcenter.com.

Library of Congress Cataloging-in-Publication Data

Names: Fitzgerald, Troy, 1968- author.
Title: Community / Troy Fitzgerald.
Description: Nampa, Idaho : Pacific Press Publishing Association, 2020. |
Summary: "A series of studies for young adults on the concept of community in the Bible"— Provided by publisher.
Identifiers: LCCN 2020007122 | ISBN 9780816366620 (paperback) | ISBN 9780816366637 (kindle edition)
Subjects: LCSH: Communities—Religious aspects—Christianity. | Communities—Biblical teaching. | Bible. Acts—Criticism, interpretation, etc. | Young adults—Religious life. | Christian life—Seventh-Day Adventist authors.
Classification: LCC BV625 .F58 2020 | DDC 250—dc23
LC record available at https://lccn.loc.gov/2020007122

April 2020

CONTENTS

INTRODUCTION

ON COMMUNITY

The word *community* describes a group that shares a common origin, life experiences, and a purpose for life's greatest endeavors. The idea of community becomes more vivid as you witness how people function in community—we will explore many examples in this devotional.

In this book, we'll consider the origins of the community in the Old Testament and move to the life of Christ. In the stories of Jesus, the community is found with the disciples, His encounters with people, and Christ's teachings.

Naturally, the idea of a church community emerges in the book of Acts, where Christianity is born. Of course, the epistles in the New Testament are letters written to the churches that are becoming a laboratory of Christian interaction. The phrase "one another" is like a code word for community, and every phrase elicits responses for real action from those who are believers.

I pray that God will be with you as you explore the concept of community in His Word.

1. ALL

*Hear, O Israel: The LORD our God,
the LORD is one.*
—Deuteronomy 6:4

Some teachers are straightforward and simply tell their students, "Read all of the questions on the test before you answer." If you are in a hurry to complete the test or if you think you already know what to do, you might miss that one key fact. On a test of forty questions, the thirty-fifth question asks, "Approximately how much does an adult female wombat weigh? The answer to this question and all the others on this test are on the wall in the hallway. Feel free to leave the room and take your test to the hallway."

You say to the teacher, "I don't understand what to do." Perhaps you forgot the process, or maybe you are being obtuse—intentionally or otherwise!

The response your teacher gives you is, "Did you read the instructions?"

When you don't know what to do, read the instructions. You should not be surprised to find that many will not read the instructions before starting.

If the conversation about community is going to be enduring, the starting point is in the complex nature of the Creator who created everything.

Before the concept of community ever became a "thing" to create or develop, there was God. Describing what life should be like, the Creator reveals that His nature is one of companionship—in the persons of the Father, Son, and Holy Spirit.

The Bible reveals the truth that "the LORD our God, the LORD is one" (Deuteronomy 6:4). If you are going to see the nature of God as an equation, your math will fail and your logic will surely become confused. An equation is a problem to solve or a concept to explain, but a truth is a statement of reality. So, if you come up with a great idea to try to convince your math teachers that one is not only one but is actually many, you might have a starting point, but you won't have a way to finish.

Count yourself blessed to be in a relationship that is greater than the parameters of your mind! For when you are at the place where you can explain the categorical reality of life accurately and completely, you have arrived! However, if you are frustrated, uneasy, stirring, wondering, thinking, hoping, imagining, and wrestling, you are at the starting point to either worship God with humility or to dive deeper into a world where you are god.

When you start trying to number the aspects of God, don't start with only one, or three, but go straight to infinity. Infinity. What do you think of when you think of the infinite God?

- God is all-knowing (omniscient)
- God is all-powerful (omnipotent)
- God is all-present (omnipresent)

When a mother looks at her baby at birth, the overwhelming response is love. Not all babies are cute—but don't tell that to a mother (seriously, don't). Love is the appropriate response. Even though we can't always explain a mother's love externally, the reality of a mother's love for her baby is obvious. In the same way, we may have difficulty explaining the infinite God to finite minds, but the evidence of His existence and nature is obvious to all who seek Him.

If you want to connect the dots or solve your conundrums about the universe, return to the passage for this reading and read all of the instructions—*carefully*.

"Hear, O Israel: The LORD our God, the LORD is one. Love the LORD your God with *all* your heart and with *all* your soul and with *all* your strength. These commandments that I give you today are to be on your hearts" (Deuteronomy 6:4–6; emphasis added).

If you want to get a handle on the nature of the Almighty, start by loving Him, reading His Word, and claiming His promises.

> In all this you greatly rejoice, though now for a little while you may have had to suffer grief in all kinds of trials. These have come so that the proven genuineness of your faith—of greater worth than gold, which perishes even though refined by fire—may result in praise, glory and honor when Jesus Christ is revealed. Though you have not seen him, you love him; and even though you do not see him now, you believe in him and are filled with an inexpressible and glorious joy, for you are receiving the end result of your faith, the salvation of your souls (1 Peter 1:6–9).

The starting point is reading the instructions in the Bible. There are, and will be, unanswered questions and mysteries that will boggle your mind—after all, the Creator is infinite. Even so, He still longs for a relationship with *you*!

INSIDE OUT

- When you think of God's attributes, which do you connect with the most?
  - God is all-knowing (omniscient)
  - God is all-powerful (omnipotent)
  - God is all-present (omnipresent)
- What part of God's nature do you think about when you pray?
- What does it mean to love with all your heart, soul, and strength?
- Consider the following texts:

  - We love because he first loved us (1 John 4:19).

  - And so we know and rely on the love God has for us. God is love. Whoever lives in love lives in God, and God in them (1 John 4:16).

  - Dear friends, let us love one another, for love comes from God. Everyone who loves has been born of God and knows God. Whoever does not love does not know God, because God is love (1 John 4:7, 8).

2. LET US

Then God said, "Let us make mankind in our image, in our likeness, so that they may rule over the fish in the sea and the birds in the sky, over the livestock and all the wild animals, and over all the creatures that move along the ground."
—Genesis 1:26; emphasis added

Us, *our*, *we*. Much like little words such as *if* and *but*, pronouns make a giant difference in a message. Typically, pronouns refer to people, and the appropriate use of a word tends to clarify the nature of the participants. When you choose words such as *I*, *me*, and *my*, the pronouns in the first person define the subject succinctly. Now, *you* is a little confusing. The audience might be *you* and you only, or it may refer to others present in the plural. But *us* and *our* and *we* can be used as "overgeneralizing" words.

Consider a few scenarios where *we* is not accurate. When a student makes a clever but inappropriate comment in class, the teacher might respond by saying, "We are not amused." In fact, several are amused, but they probably shouldn't be. A nurse or a doctor may ask a patient, "How are we feeling today?" At funerals, weddings, and graduations, the officiant or speaker often greets the audience by saying, "We are gathered here today . . . " Is the assumption that everyone is "on board" or in "one accord" about the reason for attendance?

Some people try to press their point with more authority by using the phrase, "We know from our study . . . " When they say "we," it often means *some* of the people agree with their findings.

Did people in the wild west actually say to newcomers, "We don't like strangers 'round here"? Even if someone did say those specific words, it was probably the town bully speaking. I am sure the sentiments were not unanimous. If you have ever lived in a small town, you know that newcomers are near celebrities for a while.

Even teachers and parents say, "We need to clean up the mess and put away the toys." Lies! They don't mean "we" collectively. They mean, "*You* are supposed to clean up this mess."

For our purposes, it is important to be aware of the misunderstandings caused by pronoun usage. Of all of the personal pronouns, by far, the biggest troublemaker is *we*. And yet, in the Creation story, "us" and "our" are used to reveal God's nature in creation.

"*Let us* make mankind in our image, in *our* likeness" (Genesis 1:26; emphasis added).

There are at least two ways to look at this phrase. First, the use of the phrase "Let us" implies dialogue and a choice. And second, the phrase "Let us" indicates that the whole Creation endeavor is a product of God's complete being. Consider that some of the most important things to do in life are not commanded but are the result of an intrinsic urging:

- Dear friends, *let us* love one another, for love comes from God. Everyone who loves has been born of God and knows God (1 John 4:7; emphasis added).

- Come, *let us* sing for joy to the Lord;
   let us shout aloud to the Rock of our salvation.
Let us come before him with thanksgiving
   and extol him with music and song (Psalm 95:1, 2; emphasis added).

- *Let us* draw near to God with a sincere heart and with the full assurance that faith brings, having our hearts sprinkled to cleanse us from a guilty conscience and having our bodies washed with pure water. *Let us* hold unswervingly to the hope we profess, for he who promised is faithful. And let us consider how we may spur one another on toward love and good deeds (Hebrews 10:22–24; emphasis added).

- *Let us* then approach God's throne of grace with confidence, so that we may receive mercy and find grace to help us in our time of need (Hebrews 4:16; emphasis added).

- *Let us* discern for ourselves what is right;
   let us learn together what is good (Job 34:4; emphasis added).

- *Let us* not become weary in doing good, for at the proper time we will reap a harvest if we do not give up. Therefore, as we have opportunity, let us do good to all people, especially to those who belong to the family of believers (Galatians 6:9, 10; emphasis added).

Everyone should respond to "let us."

INSIDE OUT

- How do you approach collaborative projects? Do you prefer to work with others or alone? Why?
- Consider the following texts:

  - In the past God spoke to our ancestors through the prophets at many times and in various ways, but in these last days he has spoken to us by his Son, whom he appointed heir of all things, and through whom also he made the universe. The Son is the radiance of God's glory and the exact representation of his being, sustaining all things by his powerful word. After he had provided purification for sins, he sat down at the right hand of the Majesty in heaven (Hebrews 1:1–3).

  - Above all, love each other deeply, because love covers over a multitude of sins. Offer hospitality to one another without grumbling. Each of you should use whatever gift you have received to serve others, as faithful stewards of God's grace in its various forms. If anyone speaks, they should do so as one who speaks the very words of God. If anyone serves, they should do so with the strength God provides, so that in all things God may be praised through Jesus Christ. To him be the glory and the power for ever and ever. Amen (1 Peter 4:8–11).

  - Dear friend, you are faithful in what you are doing for the brothers and sisters, even though they are strangers to you. They have told the church about your love. Please send them on their way in a manner that honors God. It was for the sake of the Name that they went out, receiving no help from the pagans. We ought therefore to show hospitality to such people so that we may work together for the truth (3 John 1:5–8).

3. NOT ALONE

The LORD God said,
"It is not good for the man to be alone.
I will make a helper suitable for him."
—Genesis 2:18; emphasis added

If you ask people to arrange the world's issues of hunger, disease, education, oppression or slavery, and loneliness from most important to least important, the responses will vary, depending on who answers. Children will often choose hunger. Because children are in the developmental stage of concrete reasoning, their solutions are usually very physical. Those in the season of midlife are keenly aware of potential disease and tend to value good health. Many in their young-adult years see an opportunity to respond to the oppression in the world, the need for education, and the importance of making strides toward improving quality of life.

The group who ranks loneliness the highest are usually those who are in their sunset years. They have negotiated seasons of poverty and plenty, weakness and vitality. They have witnessed wars, famines, the heartache that comes from despicable acts of selfishness, and heroic moments of virtue and wisdom. They have a wisdom that is not solely the product of education; they possess the wisdom that comes with experience. Those who are aging tend to choose companionship as the answer to the problem of loneliness. Challenges are going to come, but you can endure with a friend.

We are not meant to be alone. The sentiment reverberates throughout the first two chapters of Genesis. That is why Genesis 2:18 packs so much power: "It is not good for the man to be alone." Those words don't seem to belong in the perfect garden where it's "all good."

Why is being alone not good? Good is the goal, the standard of what God creates. There is more to life than just surviving. Survival is a step—but not the goal. It isn't easy; life can be a lonely place. As a human, life requires us to be alone at times. You think alone. You grow alone. Your thoughts are yours alone unless you share. You suffer alone; you cannot feel another's pain. Your salvation is yours and yours alone. When you see someone who is hungry, you can identify, but you cannot feel their hunger;

you can feel only your own. You were created to grow with other people, and the growth strengthens you—but it can also leave you devastated if the bonds of the relationship are broken.

In the Garden, the community God creates between Adam and Eve is marriage. The deeper, inherent quality of humans to be connected to others and plan for life included two people being husband and wife.

This study begins with a short quiz you can take by yourself or among friends. If you take the quiz with friends, compare your responses when you are done. Be sure to share why you answered the way you did.

Using a scale from 1 to 10 (with 1 being least important and 10 being more important), rank the qualities you most appreciate or would appreciate in a spouse:

___ Loyal	___ Responsible	___ Encouraging	
___ Hardworking	___ Selfless	___ Honest	
___ Courageous	___ Kind	___ Compassionate	___ Wise

The best thing you can do to prepare for marriage or nurture your marriage is to:

A. Become more selfless
B. Know yourself honestly
C. Develop the quality of perseverance
D. Sharpen your communication skills
E. Love Christ first

Circle the top three factors that you think keep families healthy and whole:

- Regular family worship
- Mutual respect
- Accountability
- Tolerance and forgiveness
- Common interests
- Balance between discipline and flexibility
- Communicated gratitude and appreciation
- Meaningful service
- Loyalty to each other
- High standards
- Open and honest communication
- Different interests

Now, can you substitute a friend, a coworker, someone who is going along on a church mission trip in place of a spouse? The attributes of relationships are highly transferable because we as humans were created in the image of God and made to connect with others.

INSIDE OUT

- Where have you seen evidence of God putting people in your life?
- How have you taken advantage of that heavenly appointment?
- Are there people that God is leading you to influence for His glory?
- Consider the following texts:

    - The LORD God said, "It is not good for the man to be alone. I will make a helper suitable for him" (Genesis 2:18).

    - Two are better than one,
        because they have a good return for their labor:
      If either of them falls down,
        one can help the other up.
      But pity anyone who falls
        and has no one to help them up (Ecclesiastes 4:9, 10).

    - One who has unreliable friends soon comes to ruin, but there is a friend who sticks closer than a brother (Proverbs 18:24).

4. MOTIVATION

When the woman saw that the fruit of the tree was good for food and pleasing to the eye, and also desirable for gaining wisdom, she took some and ate it. *She also gave some to her husband, who was with her,* and he ate it.
—*Genesis 3:6; emphasis added*

There was a research project many years ago that observed the behavior of monkeys in hopes of revealing a few insights on motivation. The experiment was conducted on four monkeys who were put in a room. In the center, they positioned a ladder, on top of which they placed bananas. When a monkey climbed up to reach the bananas, they were hit with a stream of cold water from the ceiling. Soaking wet, the monkey would scamper down—only to try again later. After several attempts, the monkey stopped trying. Another monkey would attempt the same approach—only to concede defeat as the others had. All four monkeys tried to reach the bananas, and all four monkeys eventually stopped attempting to climb the ladder.

Next, the researchers began replacing the monkeys one by one with a new candidate. When the newcomer would try to climb the ladder to grab a banana, the other monkeys would pull the ambitious monkey down. The other monkeys always stopped the newcomer's attempts to climb until the ambitious monkey finally gave up.

In time, the room was full of monkeys who had never been surprised with a shower of cold water because they never tried to reach the bananas. None of the monkeys would climb the ladder, but none of them knew why. While this story is likely fiction, there are lessons we can take from it.[1]

Do you know why you do what you do (or don't do)? Understanding your motivation matters. Have you ever wondered why Adam and Eve ate the fruit from the tree of knowledge of good and evil? The snake deceived Eve, and Adam took the fruit from Eve, but their motivation was different.

Why did Eve take the fruit? For some, fear lurks in thoughts of what might happen to them (violence, abandonment, failure, and so on). Others fear missing opportunities. Risk takers will try just about anything. Failing is a part of learning, and not having a chance to grow, attain, and reach out for more is painful for some. What made the fruit tempting was not the fruit itself but the lure of the missed opportunity. The snake said, "For God knows that when you eat from it your eyes will be opened, and you will be like God, knowing good and evil" (Genesis 3:5).

The deception had two parts. First, instead of embracing the truth that she was already formed in the image of her Creator, Eve bought the lie that she was not quite enough. Second, as a result of believing the first lie, the only logical pursuit was to try to be more than a child of God—to try to become God.

Adam's situation was slightly different because the snake didn't tempt him directly in the same way it seduced Eve. The text simply states, "She also gave some to her husband *who was with her*, and he ate it" (Genesis 3:6; emphasis added). In part, Adam's fall was caused by not leading well. Unfortunately, there is almost nothing written about the struggle of Adam's choice to disobey God, other than "she gave" and "I ate" (Genesis 3:12). Adam chose fellowship with Eve first, instead of putting the worship of God first. Instead of trusting in God's character, he did what he assumed he needed to do in order to not be separated from Eve.

Before the deception of the snake's ideas, Adam and Eve lived without fear. Surely the first family had heard about death, yet death had never happened; so death was a concept, not an experience. There was only a warning about one specific tree, and the consequence of eating that fruit was death.

When you experience any trauma, you store that fear in your memory, and the chemical adrenaline can tattoo the pathways in your brain. How do you react when you are afraid? Do you fight, flee, or freeze? Making bad decisions is painful. However, doing nothing has consequences as well. Understanding what motivates you helps build your relationships and engage you with your community of faith.

The fear of pain, failure, sickness, loneliness, accidents, being misunderstood, or missing a good opportunity might stop you in your tracks. And where does this fear come from? What is the antidote? There is only one answer: trusting God's character.

Eve and Adam turned their eyes away from the nature of the Creator. Whether you are dealing with seduction or cowardice, the answer for love, life, and the truth will always center on God.

Why do you run from conflict, people, challenges, or opportunities? Reflect on the way you relate to others in your life. What are your motivations, patterns, practices, hopes, and fears related to those you connect with the most? Take some time to reflect on these areas of your life.

INSIDE OUT

- How can you see and know the motivations of Adam and Eve? Are they different from yours?
- Share examples of the following:
  - Doing the right thing for the wrong reason
  - Doing the wrong thing with the right motivation
- Knowing that your sinful nature will always taint your motivations, how do you function without despair and cynicism?
- Consider the following texts:

  - The sting of death is sin, and the power of sin is the law. But thanks be to God! He gives us the victory through our Lord Jesus Christ.

  - Therefore, my dear brothers and sisters, stand firm. Let nothing move you. Always give yourselves fully to the work of the Lord, because you know that your labor in the Lord is not in vain (1 Corinthians 15:56–58).

  - Trust in the LORD with all your heart
    and lean not on your own understanding;
in all your ways submit to him,
    and he will make your paths straight.
Do not be wise in your own eyes;
    fear the LORD and shun evil (Proverbs 3:5–7).

  - Whatever you do, work at it with all your heart, as working for the Lord, not for human masters, since you know that you will receive an inheritance from the Lord as a reward (Colossians 3:23, 24).

---

1. Dario Maestripieri, "What Monkeys Can Teach Us About Human Behavior: From Facts to Fiction," *Psychology Today,* March 20, 2012, https://www.psychologytoday.com/us/blog/games-primates-play/201203/what-monkeys-can-teach-us-about-human-behavior-facts-fiction.

5. THE "IT" FACTOR

Moses listened to his father-in-law and did everything he said. *He chose capable men from all Israel and made them leaders of the people, officials over thousands, hundreds, fifties and tens. They served as judges for the people at all times. The difficult cases they brought to Moses, but the simple ones they decided themselves. Then Moses sent his father-in-law on his way, and Jethro returned to his own country.*

—Exodus 18:24–27

Do you have the "it" factor? The "it" factor is an elusive idiom that refers to the hard-to-define attribute that qualifies a person to be outstanding. Some will describe an individual as having "charisma" or "appeal," or even say someone has a "magnetic personality."[1]

Good for you if you have the "it" factor, but the rest of us will have to learn how to lead and work with people the old-fashioned way. For example, Moses is considered to be one of the greatest leaders in the Old Testament. Did Moses have the "it" factor? If you asked him, he would say, "No!" In fact, Moses cried, "Who am I that I should go to Pharaoh and bring the Israelites out of Egypt?" (Exodus 3:11).

A second time, "Moses said to the Lord, "Pardon your servant, Lord. I have never been eloquent, neither in the past nor since you have spoken to your servant. I am slow of speech and tongue" (Exodus 4:10).

Then, a third time, Moses said, "Pardon your servant, Lord. Please send someone else" (Exodus 4:13).

Those statements are not overflowing with self-confidence. Clearly, Moses learned leadership as he went along. But one particular moment became a pivotal shift for his success.

After four hundred years of slavery, the habits of thought and the natural practices of the Israelites were counter to the lifestyle of God's kingdom. The masses turned into mobs with any conflict. Disputes and arguments arose on the topics of fairness, traveling routes, food, and water. Conventional wisdom became a lightning rod for more problems to sort out until Jethro, Moses' father-in-law, made pointed observations about his leadership style.

Jethro praised God for the exodus from Egypt, but when it came to describing Moses' leadership style, he concluded, 'What you are doing is not good" (Exodus 18:17). Harsh. The assessment seems a little aggressive, but the advice was brilliant. The words offered affirmation for Moses and a better plan to lead a couple million people through the desert. Jethro offered five adjustments to Moses' approach to practice the "it" factor.

1. "It" is not about you

By default, people looked to Moses to solve their day-to-day problems. Moses spent more time dealing with conflict management than teaching the people about their God—their true Leader. After solving, serving, and helping people make restitution for bad behavior, Moses stood in the center of all the problems as the "problem solver.'

Jethro asked, "Why do you sit alone as judge, while all these people stand around you from morning till evening?" (Exodus 18:14). The situation had an easy answer, but the real power lay in evaluating Moses' effectiveness. The same is true for us. Why are you doing this work? Why are you the only one who is doing this work? How long will this continue?

The first work for leaders in community is to embrace the truth that you are not alone; don't work as though you are.

2. "It" is not whether you can do it—but whether you should

Second, step forward to do what you should do. Moses needed to focus on teaching God's will and God's way. Peace comes with knowing who you are and who you are not. Moses' decision to step back from doing everything and focus on the one thing he should do—teach—became a pivotal choice for Israel's success.

3. "It" is good to share

When you give yourself to a mission, every step builds ownership into your endeavor. Some leaders are so immersed in their work, the little tasks and big decisions culminate in their mind alone, which is expected. However, recognize that passion for your work needs to influence others in order to create a team. Moses found that being faithful to Israel's mission cultivated growth, but the only way to continue that growth was to share the leadership.

4. "It" is knowing there is another way to get the job done—trust people
If others can do the same work, you can trust them to find the best approach. When you model humility in leadership, others will value the team more than the being "in charge." When they are allowed to try, test, build, refine, and even make mistakes, the transfer of leadership that follows is thoughtful and enduring.

5. "It" is wise to listen well
After listening to Jethro, Moses acted on good advice. The Bible states, "Moses listened to his father-in-law and did everything he said" (Exodus 18:24). Listening well to counsel and then moving into action develops your team, increases the buy-in and ownership of others, and deepens a sense of confidence in your leadership. Perhaps you have the "it" factor already.

INSIDE OUT

- Reflect on the skills and abilities that God has given to you.
- What do you think is the purpose of those skills?
- How can you use and develop those gifts for the kingdom during this next week?
- Consider the following texts:
  - You then, my son, be strong in the grace that is in Christ Jesus. And the things you have heard me say in the presence of many witnesses entrust to reliable people who will also be qualified to teach others (2 Timothy 2:1, 2).
  - Humble yourselves before the Lord, and he will lift you up (James 4:10).
  - "But select capable men from all the people—men who fear God, trustworthy men who hate dishonest gain—and appoint them as officials over thousands, hundreds, fifties and tens" (Exodus 18:21).

---

1. Patty Ann Tublin, "Do You Have the 'It' Factor?" *HuffPost*, February 28, 2017, https://www.huffpost.com/entry/do-you-have-the-it-factor_b_58b5acbae4b02f3f81e44cb9.

6. THE "I" DISEASE

An unfriendly person pursues selfish ends and against all sound judgment starts quarrels.
—Proverbs 18:1

Opening your eyes to see another viewpoint has a level of risk. False teachings could deceive you. You could be swayed to question your opinions. You could be convinced to buy something you didn't originally want. You could be exposed to dangerous ideas, images, and impulses.

All of the above are possible risks of opening your mind, but they also describe what happens when you read a book, go to school or work, become a citizen of a country, commit to a particular religion, or go on a walk with a friend. The enemy outside is real, but with sound principles and the Holy Spirit to prod your conscience, you can discern the truth from the lies; the eternal from the temporary; and the good, the noble, and the beautiful from the bad.

The wisdom from the king in Proverbs is: be careful with your own preferences, biases, and unquestioned assumptions. In other words, check yourself and make sure you hear other voices as well as your own. The community needs you to look in an outward direction. To be thoughtful of others is not a denial of your internal voices and beliefs but is wise, sound judgment. A person who "seeks his own desire" (Proverbs 18:1, NKJV) is immediately contrary to the concept of community.

Jesus asked a question that was intended to teach a truth through humor, "Can the blind lead the blind? Will they not both fall into a pit?" (Luke 6:39). In Matthew's version of the teaching, Jesus warned people, "Leave them; they are blind guides" (Matthew 15:14). Maybe some individuals are determined to be "Pharisees," but most creep in that direction by slowly losing their sight. You can lose your sight and still trust a cane, a dog, a friend, and many other resources to help you function. The way you lose your vision is to ignore others and different perspectives purposefully. Being blind but thinking you can see twenty-twenty is a recipe for disaster.

Reflect on this checklist for your "sight":

- Do you avoid people you don't agree with?

- Do you check the pulse of the world around you?
- Do you ask, "Why do I believe what I believe?"
- Do you try to understand why others think differently from you?
- Do you remind yourself that what you believe today needs to grow and mature into something *more* for tomorrow?

Questions are the exercises that result in a growing mind. If your convictions and beliefs are swayed, undermined, or disillusioned by the presence of another view, it's because the muscles of your mind need a workout. Maybe that idea feels a bit extreme, but follow every dysfunction, breakdown, and destruction in life, and you will find the basic impulse to trust only yourself. You might call it an "I" disease. The "I" disease finds its roots in the human heart where everything is seen through the framework of self.

To submit to engaging another view, to allow someone else's perception to shape, craft, mold, adjust, augment, extend, add to, and color your own can create fresh insight into the world—depth perception. You can't deny the reality that your individual worldview is, by definition, small. The nature of your worldview will only grow if you expose yourself to perceptions outside of your own.

When in your life have you changed your mind?

Sometimes you simply shift your thinking instead of making a complete reversal of thought, but every adjustment makes a difference. It's wise to think, but thinking well includes thinking about other perceptions as well as your own. Adding other angles doesn't muddle the perspective but brings depth perception.

INSIDE OUT

- Was there a time when you knew that you were wrong but struggled to accept it?
- Why was it hard to change your perceptions about that reality?
- What can you do this week to develop an attitude of open-mindedness?
- Consider the following texts:

  - *The person without the Spirit does not accept the things that come from the Spirit of God* but considers them foolishness, and cannot understand them because they are discerned only through the Spirit. The person with the Spirit makes judgments about all things, but such a person is not subject to merely human judgments, for,

    "Who has known the mind of the Lord
    so as to instruct him?"
    But we have the mind of Christ (1 Corinthians 2:14–16; emphasis added).

- For this reason, ever since I heard about your faith in the Lord Jesus and your love for all God's people, I have not stopped giving thanks for you, remembering you in my prayers. I keep asking that the God of our Lord Jesus Christ, the glorious Father, may give you the Spirit of wisdom and revelation, so that you may know him better. I pray that the eyes of your heart may be enlightened in order that you may know the hope to which he has called you, the riches of his glorious inheritance in his holy people, and his incomparably great power for us who believe. That power is the same as the mighty strength he exerted when he raised Christ from the dead and seated him at his right hand in the heavenly realms, far above all rule and authority, power and dominion, and every name that is invoked, not only in the present age but also in the one to come (Ephesians 1:15–21).

- For since in the wisdom of God the world through its wisdom did not know him, God was pleased through the foolishness of what was preached to save those who believe (1 Corinthians 1:21).

7. SIMPLE MATH

Two are better than one, *because they have a good return for their labor: If either of them falls down, one can help the other up. But pity anyone who falls and has no one to help them up.*
—Ecclesiastes 4:9, 10; emphasis added

On the wall of Alex Haley's office hung a photo of a turtle sitting at the top of a post. When someone would ask about this strange picture, he would pose the obvious question, "How did a turtle get to the top of a post?" The simple answer was, "If you ever see a turtle sitting on a fence post, you know it had some help." The picture on the wall was a reminder that he, after accomplishing great things in life, didn't get there by himself—he had some help along the way.[1]

If a sense of community is inherent in God's nature, and people are created with a need and desire for others, why is there another competing compulsion to work independently of others? Is it greed? Do you want the reward all to yourself? Pride? Does your work exhibit the best version of you? Self-sufficiency? To protect and defend yourself because you are in control? Fear? Are you threatened or intimidated by others?

You can survive being alone in your work, but you can't thrive. In order for the human spirit to grow and experience the abundant life, there is a need for community, a shared endeavor.

It's true that people should work together, and sometimes life makes it necessary to reach out for help. If you are a machine and nothing can stop you from getting the job done well and fast, there is a two-letter word in that concept you should consider: *if*.

"For *if* they fall, one will lift up his companion" (Proverbs 4:10, NKJV; emphasis added).

Who plans for the "if" to show up and change everything? When planning a road trip, people will pack tools so they won't have car trouble.

Seemingly, if you prepare for the trouble, it avoids you; and if you don't, trouble will find you, usually on the side of the road. However, there is no science and no logic in manipulating the universe by your rituals. The real message is not to protect yourself from adversity but to embrace the advantage of facing any situation with another at your side. The principle applies to work, study, marriage, friendships, and spiritual growth.

The imagery of falling down and helping others up is appropriate. You can work, live, and grow independently of others. If you trip and break your ankle, you can eventually get up. Life will be difficult after the fall. Sin broke the seamless order and changed the way we grow and live. For women, the promise was, "I will make your pains in childbearing very severe; with painful labor you will give birth to children" (Genesis 3:16). For men, the ground fights them at every turn, and at the end of the day, humanity will feel the pain of struggle. In other words, at some point, you are going to fall down. It's better to have someone who can help you back up. You might be experienced, skilled, even cautious, and still fall.

Not everything you do needs colaborers because there is virtue in being an individual. The tension of being both independent and dependent finds a healthy place in being interdependent.

The way to develop the skill of interdependence is to practice asking for help and offering help. For some, it is hard to ask for help. Others struggle to be available when the overwhelming tasks of their own needs are tremendous. Practice lending and receiving a hand—it will get easier over time.

INSIDE OUT

Analyze your giving habits and reflect on the following questions:

- Do you have a sense of satisfaction in your current and past endeavors to help others?
- Could it be time to seek out some new giving opportunities?
- Do you prefer to assist quietly and anonymously, or do you find inspiration and motivation in combining your efforts with others'?
- Consider the following texts:

    - A friend loves at all times, and a brother is born for a time of adversity (Proverbs 17:17).

    - All the believers were together and had everything in common. They sold property and possessions to give to anyone who had need (Acts 2:44, 45).

    - That which was from the beginning, which we have heard, which we have seen with our eyes, which we have looked at and our hands have touched—this we proclaim concerning the Word of life. The life appeared; we have seen it and testify to it, and we proclaim to you the eternal life, which was with the Father and has appeared to us. We proclaim to you what we have seen and heard so that you also may have fellowship with us. And our fellowship is with the Father and with his Son, Jesus Christ. We write this to make our joy complete (1 John 1:1–4).

---

1. Stephen Boyd, "The Turtle on the Fence Post," Public Speaking Tips, October 21, 2011, http://www.speaking-tips.com/Articles/The-Turtle-On-The-Fence-Post.aspx.

8. TOP-TEN LIST

As iron sharpens iron,
so one person sharpens another.
—Proverbs 27:17

The proverb "iron sharpens iron" suspiciously sounds like a title on a top-ten list of popular songs. It's not just because the phrase is clever or that the metaphor seems interesting. Proverbs contain more than a few themes.

As I consider music I recognize that the theme in popular music for the past fifty years has changed significantly, but in a way, it has remained the same. The style of instruments is different, yet the lyrics describe similar values when identifying the themes from decade to decade:

- 1965: Love and escape
- 1975: Love and sex
- 1985: Lust, nostalgia, and sex
- 1995: Love and sex
- 2005: Lust and loneliness
- 2015: Love and partying

Looking at the lyrics and coding the data, you can see common themes in songwriting. Don't get lost in finding examples to corroborate the data or decry foul on behalf of your favorite decade. Literature, music, and art tend to reflect values in the culture. It is also true for the themes of the Bible.

In Matthew, you will see an emphasis on the ethics of the kingdom as a theme. Furthermore, Luke highlights topics such as forgiveness, the Holy Spirit, and joy. Mark targets the view of Christ's miracles, which shows the humanity and divine power in His actions. The audience who was listening to the king writing Proverbs clearly has a favorite theme as well: wisdom comes from listening well and taking counsel from people with experience. Listen carefully for the theme of the song:

- "The way of fools seems right to them, but the wise listen to advice" (Proverbs 12:15).
- "Where there is strife, there is pride, but wisdom is found in those who take advice" (Proverbs 13:10).

- "Plans fail for lack of counsel, but with many advisers they succeed" (Proverbs 15:22).
- "Listen to advice and accept discipline, and at the end you will be counted among the wise" (Proverbs 19:20).
- "The wise prevail through great power, and those who have knowledge muster their strength. Surely you need guidance to wage war, and victory is won through many advisers" (Proverbs 24:5, 6).

Did you hear the theme? Getting counsel and reaching out for advice is wise. Read the next few verses and listen for the theme:

- "Fools show their annoyance at once, but the prudent overlook an insult" (Proverbs 12:16).
- "A quick-tempered person does foolish things, and the one who devises evil schemes is hated" (Proverbs 14:17).
- "Whoever is patient has great understanding, but one who is quick-tempered displays folly" (Proverbs 14:29).
- "A gentle answer turns away wrath, but a harsh word stirs up anger" (Proverbs 15:1).
- "A hot-tempered person stirs up conflict, but the one who is patient calms a quarrel" (Proverbs 15:18).
- "The one who has knowledge uses words with restraint,
and whoever has understanding is even-tempered.
Even fools are thought wise if they keep silent,
and discerning if they hold their tongues" (Proverbs 17:27, 28).

Who in your life sharpens you with wisdom? The wise people in your circle usually bring people together rather than drive a wedge between them. It's not always the older one who takes the role of the sage and urges you by good counsel, although that is a common scenario. Counsel is seen in the commitment to share ideas, accountability, and to trust others to help you be better. Sometimes, the commitments are only learned by the fire of time, failure, and success. You know who sharpens you and who doesn't.

Whatever the hot-button topics or conflicts in your life today, wise people compel you to be your best. You might hear voices that use harsh words, reflect quick tempers, and make rash comments. Know that those immature impulses kill trust and can fill others with dread. Let us listen well to this song today. You will hear it if you are listening. Instead of isolation and rancor, you might find the song "Iron Sharpens Iron" will be on the top-ten list.

INSIDE OUT

Reflect on people in your life that you think of as wise:

- What are the attributes that they have in common?
- How do they make you feel when you are interacting with them?

- How can you apply the commonalities of wise people to your life?
- Consider the following texts:
    - If any of you lacks wisdom, you should ask God, who gives generously to all without finding fault, and it will be given to you. But when you ask, you must believe and not doubt, because the one who doubts is like a wave of the sea, blown and tossed by the wind (James 1:5, 6).
    - For lack of guidance a nation falls, but victory is won through many advisers (Proverbs 11:14).
    - Humble yourselves before the Lord, and he will lift you up (James 4:10).

9. RETREAT

Jesus went up on a mountainside
and called to him those he wanted,
and they came to him. He appointed twelve that they might be with him and that he might send them out to preach and to have authority to drive out demons.
—Mark 3:13–15; emphasis added

Vacation is a consuming need today. Everyone needs to stop, take a break from their routine, and cultivate the part of their soul that is fasting when they are working or studying or just managing a busy life. The value of getting away has received great attention, given the options available today. Beyond a visit to the national parks and Disneyland, there are summer camps for adults.

Yes—summer camps for adults, where adults can tap into the freedoms of childhood again. They range from the traditional kid-style summer camp activities to specialty camps to suit specific types of people—nerds, musicians, athletes, bakers, craftspeople, and more!

The purpose of getting away is as old as time—from the designation of the seventh-day Sabbath rest. The Bible offers several stories that show people who made a shift from the ordinary daily activities to enter into an extraordinary experience. Three immediately spring to mind:

- Abraham climbed a mountain.
- Moses climbed a mountain.
- Elijah climbed a mountain.

We could call these the first eco-therapy retreats.
Taking a break or going on a retreat is necessary for resetting your priorities. You will make decisions that you don't see as necessary, desirable, or even possible in the routine of daily life:

- Sometimes it's an adjustment to your goals.

- Sometimes it's the choice to start a new habit.
- Sometimes it's the decision to appreciate something you already possess but too often take for granted.
- Sometimes the retreat removes a broken idea from your mind and nudges in a better thought that produces a different perspective.

Maybe the surroundings and the landscape create a new way for you to think, feel, and wonder. The different furniture, the unfamiliar atmosphere, the lack of constant demands—changing your surroundings is a way to rest. You might be surprised to see how the constant routine drains you in a way you might not be aware of.

As Jesus entered a small team into training, their first work was to leave—to go away from the routine and begin something new. Clearly, this was not a summer camp or a reason to not work; the purpose was to shift their minds to their new relationship with Christ. They had to adjust their identity and mission as believers in Jehovah. If you have ever experienced summer camp, you remember the nuances of personality slowly revealed in your cabinmates. The disciples were a mixed group too:

- In all the lists of names, Peter is the first (Matthew 10:2–4; Mark 3:16–19; Luke 6:14–16). More is known about Peter than any other disciple, for obvious reasons: he was outspoken, he was always in action, and he always responded to Jesus in a helpful way or a dysfunctional way.
- Andrew is the brother of Peter, who broke away from the disciples of John the Baptist to follow Jesus. The Gospels record three stories in which Andrew is seeking people to bring to Jesus.
- James, the brother of John, was one of three disciples in the inner circle. A fisherman, he and his brothers were central in some of the most pivotal events of Jesus' ministry.
- John, who wrote the Gospel of John, Revelation, and three letters in the Bible, is the second most well-known of all the disciples. John and his brother James were nicknamed the Sons of Thunder, and John was considered to be the most lovable one in the bunch.
- Philip was connected to Andrew in the beginning as the disciples were called into service. There was one interaction between Jesus and Philip, where Philip was confused (John 14). I don't think this disciple was alone in his confusion, but he was the one who voiced his questions, and so history cemented his moment of uncertainty.
- Nathanael was considered by Jesus "an Israelite in whom there is no deceit" (John 1:47) Other than his initial introduction to Jesus, we don't know much about Nathanael.
- Matthew, the tax collector who dropped everything to follow Jesus, would have been an awkward inclusion to the group. Everyone hated tax collectors like Matthew, who colluded with the Romans to squeeze taxes out of the people.
- Thomas is known as the "doubting disciple" because of his need to see physical evidence for Jesus' resurrection before he would believe. However, he was also spoken of when Jesus raised Lazarus from death

and the leaders started planning to kill Jesus. When Thomas heard that Jesus was heading toward Jerusalem, this cynical follower of Jesus declared, "Let us also go, that we may die with him" (John 11:16). So he might have been a little extreme sometimes, but he was not low on faith.

- James, the lesser one—well, that's all we know about this James.
- Simon the Zealot is considered to have been in league with trained assassins who believed that the kingdom would come as they eliminated its enemies one by one. Romans were interested to know the whereabouts of zealots. Clearly, you would never assign Matthew and Simon the Zealot to the same bunk bed.
- Thaddeus—the Gospels only tell us his name.
- Judas Iscariot became Christ's betrayer in the end. However, Judas might have been the most impressive of all, from human perceptions—he was entrusted with the group's money, though that trust was misplaced.[1]

Think about the different routines, families, and expectations that were brewing in their heads when Jesus stirred them to follow Him. Now think about how God has connected you to the same mission. Look at the people in your everyday life. Not all will be your best friend. Not all will be easy to talk to. Not all will have the same motivations, but all are called to be a team.

All were invited to the retreat.

INSIDE OUT

- Why did Jesus choose twelve? Is there a significance about the number twelve?
- What did becoming one of Jesus' disciples entail?
- Were there any trained leaders from the religious establishment? Why not?
- Consider the following texts:

  - The apostles gathered around Jesus and reported to him all they had done and taught. Then, because so many people were coming and going that they did not even have a chance to eat, he said to them, "Come with me by yourselves to a quiet place and get some rest" (Mark 6:30, 31).

  - In peace I will lie down and sleep, for you alone, LORD, make me dwell in safety (Psalm 4:8).

  - But Jesus often withdrew to lonely places and prayed (Luke 5:16).

1. To read more about the Twelve Disciples, check out "Who Were the Twelve Disciples?" Bibleinfo, https://www.bibleinfo.com/en/questions/who-were-twelve-disciples#judas.

10. WITH

Jesus went up on a mountainside and called to him those he wanted, and they came to him. He appointed twelve that they might be with him *and that he might send them out to preach and to have authority to drive out demons.*
—Mark 3:13–15; emphasis added

Jesus chose disciples intentionally. It was not an accident that, most of the time, they were in a small group. Except for a few public incidents that made the headlines, Jesus taught His followers to connect on a personal level. At that time, the message of the gospel could not be mass-marketed through airwaves or satellites or social media. Jesus trusted a simple method: "They might be with him" (Mark 3:14).

If the disciples were to follow their Rabbi, their training did not resemble an all-night cramming session on the day before the test or taking a four-credit class in a one-week intensive. No, for this task, the Teacher and His students needed to take time away. Jesus offered some best practices when He said, "The student is not above the teacher, but everyone who is fully trained will be like their teacher" (Luke 6:40).

Jesus wrote His virtue on the hearts of and imprinted His instincts into a small group. The story of Christianity has been told by people who learned about their masters and one another in community. The disciples were a very mixed collection of people who absorbed and reflected the glory of His character as it shone on them.

First-century religious leaders lost sight of the value of small groups. The word *Pharisee* means "to be separated." Instead of building community, the Pharisees separated themselves from the people they were supposed to reach. The whole essence of Christianity was that it bound people to their fellows and presented them with the task of living with one another and for one another. But religious leaders had excused themselves from the table in order to not contaminate their spiritual life.

At one such table, there was Matthew, a former tax collector who was hated by Jews, sitting next to Simon the Zealot. As a Zealot, Simon was a trained killer who worked to free Israel by assassinating the enemy one person at a time. Matthew, the financial scoundrel, and Simon, the revolutionist, meeting at a café sharing their ideas about the kingdom of God! Bringing people together to be in proximity with Jesus transfers an idea: the call for the Christian life is to "do life" with one another, with people from all walks of life.

How did the community happen? The details of the day-to-day are not written in Scripture. However, it is clear that over time, the method of "being with Jesus" proved to be effective. After the Resurrection, the leaders made a remarkable observation: "When they saw the courage of Peter and John and realized that they were unschooled, ordinary men, they were astonished and they took note that *these men had been with Jesus*" (Acts 4:13; emphasis added).

It is possible to work with people and even know them well and not change your character, views, or behavior. The Savior taught by imprint, by pressing close to transfer the deepest values of heaven into His followers.

One person observed that steeping is the best way to describe the process of being a disciple of Christ—steeping instead of sampling. When making a cup of tea, you place a bag into a cup of hot water and wait. As you wait, the water permeates the bag and soaks into the contents—tea leaves and herbs packed together. The water will find a way to soak into the dry places, but it takes time. As the water permeates the bag, something wonderful happens. The water enters the bag, and what is in the bag enters the water. The more time the water and tea bag have to mingle, the stronger the flavor becomes.

The method of steeping is no trick or gimmick. It's not a "best practice" tactic you learn about at leadership seminars. The work of steeping is a natural process.

The way to steep is three-fold: being present, being aware, and being personal. Being *present* means to see what is meaningful in the moment. Being *aware* means to be conscious of the various dynamics of the situation. Being *personal* means to identify and focus on one person at a time. Ponder a few interactions in Jesus' ministry and observe the steeping approach:

- *Martha*: " 'Martha, Martha,' the Lord answered, 'you are worried and upset about many things, but few things are needed—or indeed only one. Mary has chosen what is better, and it will not be taken away from her' " (Luke 10:41, 42).
- *Mary*: " 'Leave her alone,' said Jesus. 'Why are you bothering her? She has done a beautiful thing to me. The poor you will always have with you, and you can help them any time you want. But you will not always have me. She did what she could. She poured perfume on my

body beforehand to prepare for my burial. Truly I tell you, wherever the gospel is preached throughout the world, what she has done will also be told, in memory of her' " (Mark 14:6–9).

- *Widow with two mites*: "But a poor widow came and put in two very small copper coins, worth only a few cents. Calling his disciples to him, Jesus said, 'Truly I tell you, this poor widow has put more into the treasury than all the others. They all gave out of their wealth; but she, out of her poverty, put in everything—all she had to live on.' " (Mark 12:42–44).
- *Man who had been blind from birth*: "Jesus heard that they had thrown him out, and when he found him, he said, 'Do you believe in the Son of Man?' 'Who is he, sir?' the man asked. 'Tell me so that I may believe in him.' Jesus said, 'You have now seen him; in fact, he is the one speaking with you.' Then the man said, 'Lord, I believe,' and he worshiped him." (John 9:35–38).
- *Woman healed on the Sabbath*: "The Lord answered him, 'You hypocrites! Doesn't each of you on the Sabbath untie your ox or donkey from the stall and lead it out to give it water? Then should not this woman, a daughter of Abraham, whom Satan has kept bound for eighteen long years, be set free on the Sabbath day from what bound her?' " (Luke 13:15, 16).
- *Leper who returned to give thanks*: "Jesus asked, 'Were not all ten cleansed? Where are the other nine? Has no one returned to give praise to God except this foreigner?' Then he said to him, 'Rise and go; your faith has made you well' " (Luke 17:17–19).

The community of faith requires steeping. When you are with Jesus, there is an unmistakable effect on you. Some will not understand it, but you are different because you will have been with Jesus. Others will recognize that you have been steeping.

INSIDE OUT

- What are the things that keep you from being intentionally "present" with God?
- Have there been times when you have felt distant from God?
- What are the activities that make you feel the closest to God?
- Consider the following texts:

  - The LORD your God is with you,
   the Mighty Warrior who saves.
He will take great delight in you;
   in his love he will no longer rebuke you,
   but will rejoice over you with singing (Zephaniah 3:17).

  - Don't you know that you yourselves are God's temple and that God's Spirit dwells in your midst? If anyone destroys God's temple, God will destroy that person; for God's temple is sacred, and you together are that temple (1 Corinthians 3:16, 17).

11. HERALD

Jesus went up on a mountainside and called to him those he wanted, and they came to him. He appointed twelve that they might be with him and that he might send them out to preach *and to have authority to drive out demons.*
—Mark 3:13–15; emphasis added

The telephone game was played at parties long ago. Originally, the game casually spoke to the nature of gossip and how rumors can easily change the original message. Players sit in a large circle or stand in a straight line while the first person whispers a message, which passes from one person to the next. At the end of the round, the last player tells the group what they heard, and the group compares the final phrase to the original. For example, a message that started as, "The weather outside is frightful today," by the end, had become, "Take enough time to pray for Paraguay."

For Jesus, preaching is His game plan—not a game. Before you roll your eyes and prepare yourself for some sermonizing, consider the word "preach." The original word, *kerysso*, meant to proclaim, to announce, to declare, and to herald a message.

Long ago, a king or a queen who desired to communicate with their subjects would use a herald. Without wincing or flinching at any message from the king, the herald would convey in a clear voice the desires of the establishment. The nature of the job description is a little more involved than taking notes, dictations, and being a press secretary who is the official spokesperson. Instead offering the message to others, heralds were the message. Their job description might read: You will accurately understand the king's message—in thought, tone, and emotion. Your dress, demeanor, and the way you interact with all the subjects in the kingdom represent the king.

As the herald of the king, you will you live, publicly and privately, in accordance with the virtues of the kingdom. You will live in close proximity to the king to better understand the needs and hopes for the kingdom from the standpoint of the king.

You are on call to be summoned by the king at any time. You will know the personal details of the king's life and exhibit uncompromising loyalty to his reputation.

As the herald of the king, your opinions, personal style of speaking, and the prioritization of your own preferences are never to augment or impinge on the message of the king.

Essentially, heralds were the personification of the king's message. Strangely enough, the job was considered to be one of the most respected positions in the kingdom. Would you apply for that work?

After His retreat with the newly called disciples, Jesus sent them out to "preach"; that is, to be "the King's heralds." Consider the "job description" of a herald-preacher:

- *As you go, imitate Me because most of the message is not what you say but who you are*: "The student is not above the teacher, but everyone who is fully trained will be like their teacher" (Luke 6:40).
- *As you go, know that your personal experience with Me is the most important truth to share*: "Go home to your own people and tell them how much the Lord has done for you, and how he has had mercy on you" (Mark 5:19).
- *As you go, the words you speak will be covered by a Helper to make the message clear in the minds of the hearers*: "But when they arrest you, do not worry about what to say or how to say it. At that time, you will be given what to say, for it will not be you speaking, but the Spirit of your Father speaking through you" (Matthew 10:19, 20).
- As you go, know that being authentic is more important than being pristine: "My grace is sufficient for you, for my power is made perfect in weakness" (2 Corinthians 12:9).
- *As you go, live in such a way that your words and your actions are aligned*: "Therefore everyone who hears these words of mine and puts them into practice is like a wise man who built his house on the rock" (Matthew 7:24).

You might notice that being a "dynamic speaker" or being "clever" are not required skills for the herald. In fact, everyone in the community of faith speaks on behalf of Jesus, one way or another.

INSIDE OUT

- What are some ways that God has used you in an ambassadorial role?
- How can you put yourself in a position to be prepared for that when it happens in the future?

- Consider the following texts:
    - If I speak in the tongues of men or of angels, but do not have love, I am only a resounding gong or a clanging cymbal. If I have the gift of prophecy and can fathom all mysteries and all knowledge, and if I have a faith that can move mountains, but do not have love, I am nothing. If I give all I possess to the poor and give over my body to hardship that I may boast, but do not have love, I gain nothing (1 Corinthians 13:1–3).
    - We are therefore Christ's ambassadors, as though God were making his appeal through us. We implore you on Christ's behalf: Be reconciled to God (2 Corinthians 5:20).
    - Pray also for me, that whenever I speak, words may be given me so that I will fearlessly make known the mystery of the gospel, for which I am an ambassador in chains. Pray that I may declare it fearlessly, as I should (Ephesians 6:19, 20).

12. ONE BY ONE

After this the Lord appointed seventy-two others and sent them two by two ahead of him to every town and place where he was about to go. He told them, "The harvest is plentiful, but the workers are few. *Ask the Lord of the harvest, therefore, to send out workers into his harvest field."*
—Luke 10:1, 2; emphasis added

Around the world—especially in Africa, Asia, and South America—churches share a pastor with anywhere from ten to fifty other churches. It is common to see a pastor on a motorcycle or bicycle traveling to the churches to perform a wedding, a funeral, training, or to do conflict resolution work. How can they function? How is it possible for their churches to grow?

If you look at trends from the latter part of the 1800s, church growth exploded. When the church paid pastors to "shepherd the flock," the growth stymied and slowed to a plateau. Now, there are many factors at play when describing organization trends, but it's difficult to overlook the realities today, especially in light of the growth in other parts of the world.

When people move from reporting statistics to identifying who is to blame, it never produces anything helpful. Blame is arguably one of the more advanced impulses emerging from immaturity. You can blame the organization, the liberals, the conservatives, the fundamentalists, and even the super people on the sidelines who have the problem figured out. You can blame pastors, Christian education, shortsighted leaders, and open-minded critics. You can blame this culture or that one. You can blame the men, the women, the old, or the young.

You can blame sin—that's an easier target. It's true that sin is to blame, but blaming it is not going to solve the problem. Jesus identified the problem. Matthew describes the situation, "Jesus went through all the towns and villages, teaching in their synagogues, proclaiming the good news of the kingdom and healing every disease and sickness. When he saw the crowds, he had compassion on them, because they were harassed and helpless, like sheep without a shepherd" (Matthew 9:35, 36).

The assessment? When Jesus observed the crowds of people, He witnessed "every disease and sickness" and saw that the crowds were "harassed and helpless." The crowds were a description of many, but the crowds were comprised of individuals. Furthermore, there are no shepherds that could fix the problem for the masses—for two reasons: (1) the presence of a "shepherd" can't heal every disease or affliction, and (2) the shepherds who could help point the sheep to the solution were not present and accounted for. If by "shepherds" we're talking religious leaders, they were not leading the masses. If by "shepherds" we're referencing prophets, the prophets were silent. Jesus addressed a daunting situation for people, but He still asked for a response: "The harvest is plentiful, but the *workers are few*. Ask the Lord of the harvest, therefore, to *send out workers* into his harvest field" (Luke 10:2; emphasis added).

You might hear the cynics of the board chiding the Savior's strategic plan:

- "The math doesn't add up correctly! There is no way to . . . "
- "Masterful tactic—Jesus shifts the metaphors in the middle of the conversation. What we need is a clear mission statement—we are confusing people!"
- "Here we go again. First, it's 'shepherds and sheep,' and then it is 'harvesting wheat and needing more workers.' What we need are spiritual leaders who have a business degree!"
- "We need more 'buy-in' to increase our critical mass to make the message go viral."

Jesus is the Master Teacher, so whether mixing illustrations is effective or whether Jesus needs a CEO to take the organization to the next step, He ended with a simple answer to the problem—we need more workers.

The Savior is not doing math. The masses are real people who suffer real pain. The heart of God aches for people who are lost. Consider what would happen if every believer would answer this call for more workers. The problems of the world are not going away, but the response to sin's attack would have an answer. The call for more workers has gone out. What is the response?

Guilt, shame, or fear will never muster the right motivation for gospel work. However, imagine if only a few showed up to do whatever and go wherever the Master had in mind to extend good news. Is that good? In the middle of all the metaphors, Jesus still calls for people to show up. The Bible stories have a common thread—God will accomplish the plan of salvation, and He invites people to participate in it:

- God used Abraham to move the story of redemption and restoration forward.
- God used Joseph to move to both Israelites and Egyptians forward.
- God used Esther to move her people forward.
- God used prophets such as Moses, Elijah, and Daniel to move the world forward.
- God used individuals, one by one, to move the story of redemption and restoration forward.
- God used Mary to raise His Son—who invites more workers to move the story forward.

The story can be messy, but the story is filled with flawed people who answered the call for more workers. The plan of redemption and restoration is a story of love. If you are discouraged or distracted with the apparent status quo or the seeming negative growth trends, return to the simple truth that God loves every single person on this planet. The Creator remembers every person who has lived and died. The most pressing thought in the mind of God is to impress every single heart with the invitation to be the child of God He knows them to be. And if it is true that "there will be more rejoicing in heaven over one sinner who repents" (Luke 15:7), is there any reason why you wouldn't want to answer the call for workers today? The community grows not by strategies but by increasing one by one. What do you say?

INSIDE OUT

- What skills do you think were given to you specifically for the benefit of others?
- How can you use those skills in order to grow your community of faith?
- Consider the following texts:
    - Let us not become weary in doing good, for at the proper time we will reap a harvest if we do not give up. Therefore, as we have opportunity, let us do good to all people, especially to those who belong to the family of believers (Galatians 6:9, 10).
    - Anyone who does not provide for their relatives, and especially for their own household, has denied the faith and is worse than an unbeliever (1 Timothy 5:8).
    - Do your best to present yourself to God as one approved, a worker who does not need to be ashamed, and who correctly handles the word of truth (2 Timothy 2:15).

13. COLLECTIVE FAITH

Some men came, bringing to him a paralyzed man, carried by four of them. Since they could not get him to Jesus because of the crowd, they made an opening in the roof above Jesus by digging through it and then lowered the mat the man was lying on. When Jesus saw their faith, he said to the paralyzed man, "Son, your sins are forgiven."

—Mark 2:3–5

Often, when you need to move something heavy, you get help. The more people involved, the easier it will be to move the heavy object. Just grab a handful of friends, find a corner to hold on to, and lift together. The story we'll look at in this chapter captures the essence of a community of friends who worked together to accomplish their goal. You can read the whole story in Mark 2:1–12; however focus on a few insights:

- *A collective decision.* In the story of the paralytic, someone made a choice to move an object from point A to point B—in this case, there were four individuals working together. Word soon spread through the town that Jesus, the long-expected Messiah, had arrived and informed them of where He was residing. The friends of this paralytic decided to move a man with dead weight (sorry, friend) with determination.
- *A collective problem-solving skill set.* When they carried their "package" to the house of the fisherman, everyone else had the same idea—the house was overflowing with people who were eager to see Jesus. Instead of apologizing and saying, "Well, at least we tried," or, "Sorry, we can't because of the traffic," they simply moved their friend to the roof. The effort of moving a person to the rooftop by grasping four corners of a mat was a team effort. The final step in this performance necessitated gathering the courage to remove a portion of Peter's roof. They didn't stop to analyze what Peter's reaction might be to having part of his roof removed—they just did it!

- *A collective reward.* In the story, Mark relates, "When Jesus saw their faith, he said to the paralyzed man, 'Son, your sins are forgiven' " (Mark 2:5). The friends' effort was rewarded with a double blessing. First, Jesus forgave the paralyzed man. Second, He healed him.

If you went to the doctor with a broken leg and the doctor responded by saying, "Cover your left eye and read the letters horizontally continuing toward the smallest letters," you would be unimpressed. While it seems like that is what Jesus did in forgiving the paralytic first, in reality, Jesus understood the greatest need and healed in that order—spiritual healing came first, *then* physical. In the midst of all the protests about His forgiving sins, the reality was that "Jesus saw their faith" (Mark 2:5) and immediately forgave the paralytic.

You can debate the ramifications and the theology of repentance, penitence, and the nature of confessing sins, but the four friends' faith moved Jesus to offer forgiveness *and* healing to the paralytic. The real factor is not the nature of forgiveness—but the fact that people who intercede for another move God's heart.

When you intercede, you step into the gap when others are unable to do so on their own. Interceding on behalf of another person is following Jesus' example. Praying for someone's salvation is working on God's team to lift the heavy weight of sin and guilt from their life. Asking God to work on behalf of someone in desperate need opens the floodgates of heaven.

Interceding is the work of a mediator, the high priest—it's the job description of the King of glory. The Son of God recognizes the same type of work on behalf of a friend and declares, "Greater love has no one than this: to lay down one's life for one's friends" (John 15:13). When we intercede for someone, we are figuratively laying our lives down for our friend and actively participating in Jesus' great work of intercession for us and all of humanity.

The paralytic's four friends captured community in a single act. Sometimes it requires single-mindedness—no juggling of priorities or evaluating the risk-reward ratio. The only goal is to bring a friend to the feet of Jesus—with urgency.

Is there a goal, a friend, a hope that will require a handful of friends to reach? Heaven is waiting to smile and cheer when you act on earth as they do in heaven; that's when the prayer of God is answered.

INSIDE OUT

- Take on a challenge to carry with you throughout this next week—pray a specific prayer for a friend.
- Encourage someone you see making good and meaningful decisions.

- Work to understand someone who may rub you the wrong way.
- Consider the following texts:
    - "I tell you that in the same way there will be more rejoicing in heaven over one sinner who repents than over ninety-nine righteous persons who do not need to repent" (Luke 15:7).
    - "Therefore go and make disciples of all nations, baptizing them in the name of the Father and of the Son and of the Holy Spirit" (Matthew 28:19).
    - When Moses' hands grew tired, they took a stone and put it under him and he sat on it. Aaron and Hur held his hands up—one on one side, one on the other—so that his hands remained steady till sunset (Exodus 17:12).

14. THE INNER CIRCLE

For he and all his companions were astonished at the catch of fish they had taken, and so were James and John, *the sons of Zebedee,* Simon's partners.
*Then Jesus said to Simon, "Don't be afraid; from now on you will fish for people."
So they pulled their boats up on shore, left everything and followed him.*
—Luke 5:9–11; emphasis added

One of the attributes of successful people is to distinguish the urgent from the important. A secondary attribute is possessing the courage to choose well in stressful moments. Amid the demands of a crazy day, do you take the time to distinguish the urgent from the important? What are your criteria?

For Peter, James, and John, the day started with disappointment—their efforts from the night before did not profit them. When Jesus approached them, Peter said, "Master, we've worked hard all night and haven't caught anything" (Luke 5:5). Perhaps you have days where you work all day but don't complete a thing you need to get done.

Sometimes we say it's just "one of *those* days." You know, the internet didn't work when you needed it to, the washing machine overflowed, your favorite shirt shrank after it went through the dryer, and supper ended up looking more like charcoal than food. When one circus settles down to the point of manageability, another one starts up. You deal with each issue as it arises, but at the end of the day, you feel defeated. Nothing you wanted to happen happened.

These potential disciples of Jesus are not surprised by their failure—it's fishing, it happens. What is not expected is that when His sermon ends, the Teacher asks them to try fishing again. The greatest catch of the century occurred after clock-out time. Then, after experiencing a profitable fishing moment, Jesus asks them to sell out and follow Him.

And they did. Their relationship as business partners had had good days and bad days, but after following Jesus, fishing was child's play. Instead of boats, nets, and fish, the blind could see, the deaf could hear, leprosy was cleansed, demons were banished, hungry crowds of people were fed, and angry synagogue leaders were affronted. Every day there was something new.

Peter, James, and John were among Jesus' twelve disciples, but they were also the three members of "the inner circle." You might think that Jesus' having an inner circle is inappropriate, that choosing only three to be in that inner circle is unfair. But if you think about your personal life, you'll realize that you have an inner circle.

When you look at your inner circle, how did your group come to be formed? Perhaps it was common experiences or personal affinity. Sometimes it's a work situation or shared child-rearing experiences that connect people together through common goals and activities.

In the four Gospels, there are three special events that the inner circle experienced. The first event happened at Jairus's house. When Jairus asked Jesus to come and heal his daughter, they began the trek with one interruption after another. Then, while they were still on the way, messengers came to tell Jairus, "Your daughter is dead" (Mark 5:35).

In this situation, one might offer comfort and care while the family grieves. However, Jesus pressed into the house and "He did not let anyone follow him except Peter, James and John the brother of James" (Mark 5:37).

Imagine the scene inside the house. The stress increases as Jesus says, "The child is not dead but asleep" (Mark 5:39). Then the impossible words become a reality—the little girl returns to life. For Peter, James, and John, a successful daytime fishing expedition is one thing, but watching Jesus speak life back into a dead girl is truly stunning!

The second time the inner circle was called to a special meeting involved a hike up a mountain. "After six days Jesus took Peter, James and John with him and led them up a high mountain, where they were all alone. There he was transfigured before them. His clothes became dazzling white, whiter than anyone in the world could bleach them" (Mark 9:2, 3).

The presence of Moses and Elijah was impressive, but then the voice of God spoke, "This is my Son, whom I love. Listen to him!" (Mark 9:7). Imagine witnessing Jesus' supernatural power, seeing revered prophets, and hearing God's voice—what an awesome moment in human experience!

The third excursion involved an appeal for these three friends to come and pray for Him. "They went to a place called Gethsemane, and Jesus said to his disciples, 'Sit here while I pray.' He took Peter, James and John along with him, and he began to be deeply distressed and troubled. 'My soul is overwhelmed with sorrow to the point of death,' he said to them. 'Stay here and keep watch' " (Mark 14:32–34).

To see, hear, and feel all of the experiences of Jesus casting out demons, feeding people, teaching, and speaking to storms would have been amazing to witness. But all of those experiences came down to this time of prayer.

From the standpoint of the inner circle, it's inconceivable to see their Rabbi, Messiah, and Lord diminished with grief and unimaginable horror. Where is the voice of God now? Where is the confident command for an astounding miracle? Where are the answers to all the questions?

When you go through the fire with a small group of companions, you experience the central idea of church. Jesus did not play favorites but ignited three to start a fire that continues today.

INSIDE OUT

- Who are the people in your inner circle?
- How does your inner circle function, and what are the strengths and weaknesses of your small community?
- How can you see God's hand in the way the members of your inner circle experience life with you?
- Consider the following texts:

    - When Job's three friends, Eliphaz the Temanite, Bildad the Shuhite and Zophar the Naamathite, heard about all the troubles that had come upon him, they set out from their homes and met together by agreement to go sympathize with him and comfort him (Job 2:11).

    - One who has unreliable friends soon comes to ruin, but there is a friend who sticks closer than a brother (Proverbs 18:24).

    - Walk with the wise and become wise, for a companion of fools suffers harm (Proverbs 13:20).

15. ACTS 1:8-JERUSALEM

Then they gathered around him and asked him, "Lord, are you at this time going to restore the kingdom to Israel?"
He said to them: "It is not for you to know the times or dates the Father has set by his own authority. But you will receive power when the Holy Spirit comes on you; *and you will be my witnesses in Jerusalem, and in all Judea and Samaria, and to the ends of the earth."*
—Acts 1:6–8; *emphasis added*

What began as an ordinary day ended with a huge surprise. Do you like surprises? The common answer is, "It depends on the surprise." When the disciples gathered on the hill, the question on everyone's mind was, "What is going to happen next?"

Surprises: An unexpected visitor at your door. Showing up for class ready for a lecture only to find there is a test. Police car lights in your rearview mirror get your attention. When someone suggests you sit down before the conversation begins, you immediately wonder what has happened. It doesn't take much to shift the conversation from ordinary banter to a pivotal moment with one announcement. If you've had an average day turn into a major event, you might imagine how the disciples felt when Jesus shifted the conversation from a normal class discussion to, "By the way, I'm leaving for heaven in a few minutes, so listen carefully."

The disciples immediately asked about the future. "Lord, are you at this time going to restore the kingdom to Israel?" (Acts 1:6). When they asked that question, the conversation changed. Jesus altered the focus completely in one sentence: "But *you will receive power* when the *Holy Spirit comes on you*; and *you will be my witnesses*" (Acts 1:8; emphasis added).

After the shock and commotion of the announcement, Jesus ascended into heaven. To add to that memorable day, two angels appeared to the disciples. "They were looking intently up into the sky as he was going, when suddenly two men dressed in white stood beside them. 'Men of Galilee,' they said, 'why do you stand here looking into the sky? This same Jesus, who has been taken from you into heaven, will come back in the same way you have seen him go into heaven' " (Acts 1:10, 11).

As the events of the day settled into conscious reality, the disciples were arrested by the plan. They had been trained. The instructions were clear: "You will be my witnesses in Jerusalem, and in all Judea and Samaria, and to the ends of the earth" (Acts 1:8).

In the coming pages, you will see snapshots of the work of the Holy Spirit in creating a community of believers. These believers will surprise the world with their stories of miracles, kindness, generosity, and a single-minded mission to testify about Jesus. Some of the events will be so sensational they challenge believability. Other moments are raw and gritty.

If there is one takeaway from the story of the first church—the community of believers—it is this key phrase, "You will be my witnesses" (Acts 1:8). A witness is someone who experienced something firsthand and is willing to take a stand and speak.

Witnesses speak about what, specifically? The one theme repeated in every description, sermon, and story in Acts is the resurrection of Jesus from the dead. "With great power the apostles continued to testify to the resurrection of the Lord Jesus" (Acts 4:33).

Today, the reason to follow Jesus comes down to the fact He defeated death for all. The parables about ethics and forgiveness are insightful. The compassion and kindness for those who suffer is inspiring. The uncompromising loyalty, even when people were cruel, was heroic. The theological ramifications of the existence of God are arguable and compelling because of the life of Christ.

Today, if you believe—why do you? What is it about Jesus that moves you stand up and say, "I believe"? Remember Peter's response when Jesus asked who the disciples thought He was? Peter declared, "You are the Messiah, the Son of the living God" (Matthew 16:16).

In response to Peter's declaration, Jesus said, "And I tell you that you are Peter, and on this rock, I will build my church, and the gates of Hades will not overcome it" (Matthew 16:18). Jesus is the true foundation—the Rock—the church is built upon.

Community starts when you speak up and testify. Don't worry about being polished or having a sizzling story about how your lifestyle has had a complete turnabout. Some will shy away from speaking up because they might think

- *I don't know enough,*
- *I don't always follow,*
- *I struggle with problems, habits, or issues every day*, or
- *I don't feel like this is real.*

Our testimony is a story that demonstrates our daily growth in knowing Christ. Remember, the woman at the well said, "Come, see a Man who told me all things that I ever did. Can this be the Christ?" (John 4:29, NKJV). You might say, "Where is the testimony? Her declaration is not complete." Consider the simple observation and invitation in the woman's question. As a result of that short, unrefined, and incomplete version of one conversation, her question started a revival: "Many of the Samaritans from that town believed in him because of the woman's testimony, 'He told me everything I ever did' " (John 4:39).

Your present sphere of influence is the beginning point for sharing the gospel. The church starts when you testify. Right here. Right now.

INSIDE OUT

- This week, ask the Holy Spirit to help you recognize opportunities to share the good news with someone else.
- This week, pray for courage to step out of the comfort of easy conversation and dive into eternal topics.
- This week, ask for discernment to listen for and to speak boldly about God's grace in your life.
- This week, invite God to introduce you to someone whom you would never think to reach out to unless you were impressed by the Holy Spirit.
- Which testimony from the following list compels you the most? Why?

    - My mouth will tell of your righteous deeds,
of your saving acts all day long—
though I know not how to relate them all.
I will come and proclaim your mighty acts, Sovereign Lord;
I will proclaim your righteous deeds, yours alone (Psalm 71:15, 16).

    - As Jesus was getting into the boat, the man who had been demon-possessed begged to go with him. Jesus did not let him, but said, "Go home to your own people and tell them how much the Lord has done for you, and how he has had mercy on you" (Mark 5:18, 19).

    - I will declare your name to my people; in the assembly I will praise you (Psalm 22:22).

    - Come and hear, all you who fear God; let me tell you what he has done for me (Psalm 66:16).

    - It is my pleasure to tell you about the miraculous signs and wonders that the Most High God has performed for me (Daniel 4:2).

16. ACTS 1:8-JUDAEA AND SAMARIA

"But you will receive power when the Holy Spirit comes on you; and you will be my witnesses *in Jerusalem, and in all Judea and Samaria, and to the ends of the earth."*

—Acts 1:8; *emphasis added*

In law, you will find many types of witnesses in court: lay witnesses, eyewitnesses, character witnesses, hostile witnesses, or expert witnesses. Often the expert witness causes the most concern because they are rigorously vetted for credibility, and they can speak to what they think is true and accurate as pertains to their field of study.

Is it possible that believers shy away from sharing their story because they don't think they fit the criteria for being "expert witnesses"? When a handful of young adults were discussing the idea of sharing their testimony, they shared with me the following:

- "My testimony is pretty short. I don't have great stories, just a lot of evidence that God's Son is the only way home."
- "I believe that Jesus has brought me through so much, but I don't think my story would help someone."
- "I have more questions than I have answers."
- "My walk with Christ is either on a high mountain seeing everything clearly or in the pit, at the bottom of a swamp, drowning in mud—I want more consistency between the Lord and me."

When pressed for more specific responses to life's greater questions, their answers were alive with details, opinions, experiences, and even passionate convictions about their relationships with Christ. Perhaps the initial obstacle is the definition of a testimony. There is work to be done in sharing within our community of faith.

Jesus gave His last charge to the disciples with clear instructions: "Go be witnesses." Years later, Peter counseled fellow believers to continue being witnesses when he wrote, "Always be prepared to give an answer to everyone who asks you to give the reason for the hope that you have. But do this with gentleness and respect, keeping a clear conscience" (1 Peter 3:15, 16). Also, consider that every testimony is unique. You might feel like your journey is not compelling or helpful. For now, consider a few examples from the Bible, then temper and expand the way you share your story with others, and see if it helps.

- Asaph, in Psalm 73, describes a season where he grew cynical and envious of the prosperity the wicked were enjoying. The story is powerful because to recalibrate his mind, he went to the sanctuary.

  "When I tried to understand all this,
  it troubled me deeply
  till I entered the sanctuary of God;
  then I understood their final destiny" (Psalm 73:16, 17).

  The end of the song is not about "everything is better now," but "my heart sees the bigger picture."
- King Nebuchadnezzar, ruler of the known world, declares in Daniel 4, "It is my pleasure to tell you about the miraculous signs and wonders that the Most High God has performed for me" (Daniel 4:2). The king's testimony is one of the hallmark experiences of going from the best to the worst—and through the experience he learns about and later testifies about God's authority and goodness.
- The demoniac, when released from the oppression of demons, tried to stay close to Jesus, but the Savior charged him, " 'Go home to your own people and tell them how much the Lord has done for you, and how he has had mercy on you.' So the man went away and began to tell in the Decapolis how much Jesus had done for him. And all the people were amazed" (Mark 5:19, 20).
- Even the young man who was born blind was asked about this questionable healer who healed on the Sabbath. In answer to the Pharisees, he declared, "Whether he is a sinner or not, I don't know. One thing I do know. I was blind but now I see" (John 9:25).

Clearly, if there are rules to sharing your testimony, they need to be the following:

- *Personal:* You are using yourself as evidence of what God has done in your life.
- *Natural*: Sometimes the situation calls for a few words and in other situations you should spend time to share more, but the wisdom and the work of the Holy Spirit is your guide.
- *Pivotal*: Whatever you have experienced, your story is most compelling when you describe how your life has been altered or even changed by knowing Christ.

As we journey through the snapshots of community in Acts, you will read stories and hear testimonies and find your place in the community of faith.

INSIDE OUT

- If you had to tell someone in fewer than twenty words why you follow Christ as Lord and Savior, what would you say?
- Speak, write, or reflect on three moments in your life that changed your relationship with God.
- Pray a prayer of thanksgiving for the pivotal moments in your life when God has spoken to you.
- Consider the following texts:

    - So do not be ashamed of the testimony about our Lord or of me his prisoner. Rather, join with me in suffering for the gospel, by the power of God (2 Timothy 1:8).

    - For I am not ashamed of the gospel, because it is the power of God that brings salvation to everyone who believes: first to the Jew, then to the Gentile (Romans 1:16).

    - For in him you have been enriched in every way—with all kinds of speech and with all knowledge— God thus confirming our testimony about Christ among you (1 Corinthians 1:5 6).

17. ACTS 1:8–ENDS OF THE EARTH

"But you will receive power when the Holy Spirit comes on you; and you will be my witnesses in Jerusalem, and in all Judea and Samaria, and to the ends of the earth."
—Acts 1:8; emphasis added

If you want to see a frustrated person, watch one who is trying to assemble a toy late on Christmas Eve while trying to follow instructions written in tiny print.

While it's true that instructions are not always clear, in recent years, graphic designers have started creating clever instructions meant to entertain. Designers of instructions are having fun with their consumers in an attempt to liven things up. Many of the instructions written on labels are to protect the company from lawsuits. If we look around our world, we see instructions everywhere.

At the Ascension, Jesus gave final instructions to the disciples, but unlike some of the instructions we'll come across in life, these are clear. The believers were to testify first in Jerusalem; then in Judaea and Samaria; and, finally, to the ends of the earth. It's important to start sharing your testimony with those you are closest to. From there, expand your circle in a growing sphere of influence.

Again, the disciples asked specifically, "Lord, are you at this time going to restore the kingdom to Israel?" (Acts 1:6). You can't separate Judaism from the story of Christianity. The story of salvation started in the Garden; progressed through the story of Abraham's family, which eventually became a nation; and grew to include all of the followers of Jesus around the world.

The Gospels share a variety of stories in which Jesus taught, ate and drank with, and healed many people in regions that were not primarily Jewish. His instructions to preach the gospel first in Jerusalem; then in Judaea and Samaria; and, finally, to the ends of the earth shouldn't be a surprise to His followers.

The good news of the risen Christ found many listeners in Jerusalem.

Judaea and Samaria were neighbors, but relationships were strained because of centuries of division and prejudice—but the gospel brought healing where there had been brokenness. The gospel would find open hearts everywhere because the time was right, the message was right, and the Person was the right answer for humanity's problems.

God knew when the timing was perfect and, "when the set time had fully come, God sent his Son, born of a woman, born under the law, to redeem those under the law, that we might receive adoption to sonship. Because you are his sons, God sent the Spirit of his Son into our hearts, the Spirit who calls out, 'Abba, Father.' So you are no longer a slave, but God's child; and since you are his child, God has made you also an heir" (Galatians 4:4–7).

If you ever become frustrated by the complicated suggestions and answers for the meaning of life tossed around by the world, scan through the Bible. The story line of Scripture makes more sense than any other message today. Not only is the story of the Bible consistent and enduring, the story of God and His people is beautiful.

After the Resurrection, the good news of Christ went viral. Silly stories and hoaxes will vanish with the fire of persecution, but real movements continue despite opposition. Critics spoke out, and the enemies were in power, yet the story of God's redemptive secret weapon shared the antidote for death.

Still today, there are millions around the world testifying—witnessing to the old story. "You will be my witnesses in Jerusalem, and in all Judea and Samaria, and to the ends of the earth" (Acts 1:8).

Out of all the instructions in the world, Jesus' words still make sense.

INSIDE OUT

- Think of the words *pastor*, *minister*, and *evangelist*. Reflect on things that come to mind when you think of each word.
- What are the differences between the roles those titles represent?
- How can you integrate those roles in your day-to-day life?
- Consider the following texts:
    - "Then I will give you shepherds after my own heart, who will lead you with knowledge and understanding" (Jeremiah 3:15).
    - "Keep watch over yourselves and all the flock of which the Holy Spirit has made you overseers. Be shepherds of the church of God, which he bought with his own blood" (Acts 20:28).
    - "I will place shepherds over them who will tend them, and they will no longer be afraid or terrified, nor will any be missing," declares the LORD (Jeremiah 23:4).

18. PENTECOST

When the day of Pentecost came, they were all together in one place.

—Acts 2:1

If you were to pick five events in the Bible that you consider the most pivotal, which would you choose? Here are some of my suggestions:

- Creation
- The Fall
- The Exodus
- The birth of Jesus
- The Crucifixion and Resurrection

As I was compiling this list, I had to wonder, *Should I include the Day of Pentecost on the list?* Some have observed that Pentecost is the complete opposite of what happened at the construction of the Tower of Babel. At the Tower of Babel, the people's purpose was summed up in these words: "So that we may make a name for ourselves" (Genesis 11:4). At Pentecost, the believers were to be witnesses to the God of power. At Babel, God decided to "confuse their language so they [would] not understand each other" (Genesis 11:7). At Pentecost, even though they were speaking different languages, each person could understand the message in their own tongue (Acts 2:8). At Babel, they were confounded in disunity, but at Pentecost, "all the believers were together and had everything in common" (Acts 2:44). At Babel, God scattered the people to the four corners of the earth (Genesis 11:8). At Pentecost, the people gathered in one place and were sent out with one message to the world. At Babel, the people tried to build a tower that would reach the heavens, but at Pentecost, they gathered, waiting for heaven to come down to them. At Babel, the people initiated their effort to achieve their desires, but at Pentecost, God sent the gift of the Holy Spirit, and the people received repentance and salvation. Pentecost is a key event in the Bible!

So why did the people gather together on that day? One reason they gathered was in response to the reality of the *resurrection* of Jesus. Pentecost (fifty days after the Passover) was the great send-off for the news of the risen Christ to go to the world! The Resurrection was the key focus of every sermon. Everyone had heard rumors about the risen Christ and what that news meant for all—now they listened as witnesses shared what they had seen and experienced. Paul writes about the early believers and what compelled them to become Christians: "For what I received I passed on to you as of first importance: that Christ died for our sins according to the Scriptures, that he was buried, that he was raised on the third day according to the Scriptures, and that he appeared to Cephas, and then to the Twelve. After that, he appeared to more than five hundred of the brothers and sisters at the same time, most of whom are still living, though some have fallen asleep. Then he appeared to James, then to all the apostles" (1 Corinthians 15:3–7).

A second reason why people gathered had to do with the *promise* Jesus made many months before. In fact, the promise for the outpouring of God's Spirit is in the Old Testament, as well:

> "And afterward,
>   I will pour out my Spirit on all people.
> Your sons and daughters will prophesy,
>   your old men will dream dreams,
>   your young men will see visions.
> Even on my servants, both men and women,
>   I will pour out my Spirit in those days" (Joel 2:28, 29).

After His resurrection, Jesus made this shocking statement: "I am going to leave." However, the Comforter, the very Spirit of God, would come as promised, exactly on time.

- "And I will ask the Father, and he will give you another advocate to help you and be with you forever—the Spirit of truth" (John 14:16).
- "When the Advocate comes, whom I will send to you from the Father—the Spirit of truth who goes out from the Father—he will testify about me" (John 15:26).
- "But very truly I tell you, it is for your good that I am going away. Unless I go away, the Advocate will not come to you; but if I go, I will send him to you" (John 16:7).

Even though the disciples couldn't imagine the event of Pentecost before it happened, they experienced the gift unmistakably.

The third reason why they gathered is because they were to *wait for God's time to arrive*. You can imagine how difficult it would be to wait, yet their Savior told them, "Do not leave Jerusalem, but *wait* for the gift my Father promised" (Acts 1:4; emphasis added). Jesus informed the disciples that God's timing would determine the next great event, but they would need to be ready when "the Holy Spirit comes on you" (Acts 1:8). Regardless of all of their unanswered questions about the future, the disciples remained attentive to God's promise.
Let's read the whole story:

> When the day of Pentecost came, they were all together in one place. Suddenly a sound like the blowing of a violent wind came

from heaven and filled the whole house where they were sitting. They saw what seemed to be tongues of fire that separated and came to rest on each of them. All of them were filled with the Holy Spirit and began to speak in other tongues as the Spirit enabled them. . . .

. . . Amazed and perplexed, [the listeners] asked one another, "What does this mean?" (Acts 2:1–4, 12).

Pentecost is like the birthday of the Christian church. It was at that time that the church moved from a gathering to a full-on gospel movement. Instead of trying to parse out the various parts and angles of the outpouring of the Holy Spirit, perhaps it would be better to embrace the whole story. In the end, consider the question the listeners asked: "What does this mean?"

INSIDE OUT

- Do you think that the Holy Spirit is as active today as He was in Acts? How?
- How can you identify the Spirit's power in a believer's life?
- How can you see evidence in a seeker searching for God? What are the signs of a desire for God?
- Consider the following texts:

    - "But the advocate, the Holy Spirit, whom the Father will send in my name, will teach you all things and will remind you of everything I have said to you" (John 14:26).

    - But the fruit of the Spirit is love, joy, peace, forbearance, kindness, goodness, faithfulness, gentleness and self-control. Against such things there is no law (Galatians 5:22, 23).

    - In the same way, the Spirit helps us in our weakness. We do not know what we ought to pray for, but the Spirit himself intercedes for us through wordless groans (Romans 8:26).

    - After they prayed, the place where they were meeting was shaken. And they were all filled with the Holy Spirit and spoke the word of God boldly (Acts 4:31).

19. BELIEVERS IN ACTS 2 AND 5

They devoted themselves to the apostles' teaching and to fellowship, to the breaking of bread and to prayer. Everyone was filled with awe at the many wonders and signs performed by the apostles. All the believers were together and had everything in common. They sold property and possessions to give to anyone who had need. Every day they continued to meet together in the temple courts. They broke bread in their homes and ate together with glad and sincere hearts, praising God and enjoying the favor of all the people. And the Lord added to their number daily those who were being saved.

—*Acts 2:42–47; emphasis added*

Usually, when describing the characteristics of something, someplace, or someone, you can convey the message in a short list. Although nine seems like a rare number for a list of characteristics, when Luke portrayed the church, he describes the community of faith with nine characteristics:

1. A *learning community*: "They devoted themselves to the apostles' teaching" (Acts 2:42). The early church paints a picture of a community who is hungry and thirsty for understanding and participating in God's plan for saving people. Not everyone has the same experience, but everyone is moving toward the same goal.

2. A *fellowshiping community*: "[And they devoted themselves] to fellowship" (Acts 2:42). The shared experience comes from spending time together in

close proximity and learning to do life together. It includes activities as simple as eating together or working on projects together.

3. *A praying community*: "[They were devoted] to prayer" (Acts 2:42). Prayer is a nonnegotiable reality for developing a relationship with God. Praying involves listening, asking for help, offering praise and thanksgiving, interceding for others, admitting you are broken, and declaring what you believe or hope.

4. *An awe-filled community*: "Everyone was filled with awe" (Acts 2:43). The believers sensed God's presence in everyday life. Believers who are attuned to recognizing the holiness of God as His glory shines on them will be filled with awe and wonder.

5. *A happening community*: "Many wonders and signs [were] performed by the apostles" (Acts 2:43). In this community, miracles were a common occurrence. Clearly, the believers were amazed (but not surprised) by the miraculous.

6. *A generous community*: "They sold property and possessions to give to anyone who had need" (Acts 2:45). Every good thing in your life is a gift from God; this fact makes it easier to share with others. Those who follow the risen Christ will give to others in need with a cheerful heart, always.

7. *A worshiping community*: "Every day they continued to meet together in the temple courts" (Acts 2:46). A believing community will dedicate time, space, and effort to demonstrate "God's worth" together. The Holy Spirit arrests the minds and hearts of people when they dedicate time for worshiping alongside one another.

8. *A happy community*: "They broke bread in their homes and ate together with glad and sincere hearts" (Acts 2:46). Clearly, this church knew how to laugh, sing, and live life with a sense of celebration—in all circumstances. Surely, not everything was a party, yet in even the worst moments, they *lived with hope*.

9. *A community that would attract others*: They were "praising God and enjoying the favor of all the people" (Acts 2:47). Surely, if the first marks of the church are real and consistent in your life, the obvious result will be growth. People saw the power of God in everyday life and finally saw something to believe in and give their lives to.

The marks of the community of faith are obvious, compelling, and enduring. What a sight to see! Imagine what it would look like in your city? Comparing the local church today to the early church is not fair. However, the gospel of Christ and the gift of the Holy Spirit are the same. The opportunity to leverage your life for the cause of Christ is available today. Review the list of characteristics and ask: "Does the world need this type of church today?"

INSIDE OUT

- What are attributes within our communities that are the rarest today?
- What is the most effective attribute of the church today?
- If you wanted to see the most growth in your community of faith, what is something that you can intentionally focus on to make that growth happen?
- What characteristic is most needed today?
- What characteristic is most difficult to maintain over time?
- What characteristic requires the most risk personally from the believers?
- Consider the following texts:

    - I appeal to you, brothers and sisters, in the name of our Lord Jesus Christ, that all of you agree with one another in what you say and that there be no divisions among you, but that you be perfectly united in mind and thought (1 Corinthians 1:10).

    - Live in harmony with one another. Do not be proud, but be willing to associate with people of low position (Romans 12:16).

    - Whatever happens, conduct yourselves in a manner worthy of the gospel of Christ (Philippians 1:27).

20. GREAT EXPECTATIONS

When he saw Peter and John about to enter, he asked them for money. Peter looked straight at him, as did John. Then Peter said, "Look at us!" So the man gave them his attention, expecting to get something from them. Then Peter said, "Silver or gold I do not have, but what I do have I give you. In the name of Jesus Christ of Nazareth, walk."

—Acts 3:3–6

Expectations are powerful. When Jesus made startling and seemingly unbelievable statements, the disciples must have had high expectations. For instance, when Jesus said, "Very truly I tell you, whoever believes in me will do the works I have been doing, and they will do even greater things than these, because I am going to the Father" (John 14:12), the disciples must have wondered, *Is Jesus serious?* Sometimes people try to motivate others to do their best by hyperbole, but that wasn't Jesus' method. So does He really expect His followers to do what He did? Let's review:

- Jesus healed people who were blind, deaf, lame, leprous, and had other physical dysfunctions.
- Jesus banished all demons from people who were possessed.
- Jesus produced food for those who were hungry.
- Jesus raised the dead to life.

Jesus' statement that His followers will do the same works He did while on earth is not based on our strength or power, nor is it an overstatement of His expectations. The work Jesus did is your job today. But there is more. Jesus added that His followers would do greater works than His. How can you top healing, exorcisms, food service, and raising the dead?

The key is what you should expect to do and through whose power you will be able to achieve these things. This extraordinary claim about you is only possible because Jesus is going to leave, because He is "going to the Father" (John 14:12). In John 14 through 16, Jesus unpacks the gift and the promise of the Holy Spirit to the disciples. The expectations are real. It's not a trick to psychologically manipulate you into trying to do good yet impossible things—this is the master plan.

When Jesus was present in the flesh, He could be in Jerusalem or Galilee—but not both. The gift of the Holy Spirit equips all of us to do the same work because, through the Spirit, Christ dwells inside each believer.

It's true! In fact at Pentecost, three thousand disciples went home with Holy Spirit power. The story at the temple gate is another moment when the prophecy made became a promise kept. The beggar expected a few coins to sustain his survival. What else could he hope for?

Humbled by God's master plan, Peter offers the one thing he possesses—the indwelling Christ. The law of expectation is evident by the fact that Peter, without hesitation, "[took] him by the right hand, he helped him up, and instantly the man's feet and ankles became strong" (Acts 3:7).

Clearly, everyone is on their feet, cheering, and praising God. It's a miracle! Peter reminds the audience, "Fellow Israelites, why does this surprise you? Why do you stare at us as if by our own power or godliness we had made this man walk? . . . By faith in the name of Jesus, this man whom you see and know was made strong. It is Jesus' name and the faith that comes through him that has completely healed him, as you can all see" (Acts 3:12, 16).

Could you expect more from this day? Is it possible that many still hope only to receive a few coins or some crumbs? Perhaps it's time to open your hands and expect more.

INSIDE OUT

- What would it look like if you went through the next couple of days in expectation of the Holy Spirit working in, by, or through you?
- If you could ask for the Holy Spirit's help with something knowing it would be done, what would you ask for?
- What value do you see in a community that is expecting the Holy Spirit to work in it?
- Consider the following texts:
    - "Very truly I tell you, whoever believes in me will do the works I have been doing, and they will do even greater things than these, because I am going to the Father" (John 14:12).

- “For the Father loves the Son and shows him all he does. Yes, and he will show him even greater works than these, so that you will be amazed” (John 5:20).

- As a result, people brought the sick into the streets and laid them on beds and mats so that at least Peter’s shadow might fall on some of them as he passed by (Acts 5:15).

21. WISE COUNSEL

Peter and the other apostles replied: "We must obey God rather than human beings! The God of our ancestors raised Jesus from the dead—whom you killed by hanging him on a cross. God exalted him to his own right hand as Prince and Savior that he might bring Israel to repentance and forgive their sins. We are witnesses of these things, and so is the Holy Spirit, whom God has given to those who obey him." When they heard this, they were furious and wanted to put them to death.

—Acts 5:29–33

Perhaps you have seen the headlines before:

- "Overzealous Parents Ruin Little League Game"
- "Road Rage Causes Wreck"
- "Senseless Acts of Violence on Black Friday"

Maybe you have even experienced moments when people are seething with anger, furious at the store, fuming about someone who is taking too much time "getting out of the way," or taking too much time to get the job done. Today, tempers seem more volatile than ever.

In this Acts 5 snapshot of the early church community, the apostles were imprisoned for their loyalty to the story of Jesus. The Sanhedrin, the group responsible for performing the initial investigation, was quickly overcome by anger. Why? Essentially, although the apostles of Jesus were arrested and put in prison, an angel opened the doors and set them free. Instead of sharpening their knives for justice, the Sanhedrin learned about a revival taking place in the temple because their would-be prisoners were preaching there. The Bible states, "When they heard this, they were furious and wanted to put them to death" (Acts 5:33).

Before you consider the advice of Gamaliel, who urged the leaders to practice restraint, first reflect on a few insights about the Sanhedrin.

The Sanhedrin was created in the spirit of God's sense of justice and mercy. The Jewish legal system was created to protect the accused, even if the accused were indeed guilty. The idea of "innocent until proven guilty" is based on principles found in the Old Testament. The purpose of their justice system's "eye for eye" (Exodus 21:24) was meant to deter vengeance, not to legitimize the act of revenge.

In the heat of the moment, Gamaliel brings wisdom back to the Sanhedrin by suggesting the following, "Therefore, in the present case I advise you: Leave these men alone! Let them go! For if their purpose or activity is of human origin, it will fail. *But if it is from God, you will not be able to stop these men;* you will only find yourselves fighting against God" (Acts 5:38, 39; emphasis added).

Gamaliel was "a teacher of the law, who was honored by all the people" (Acts 5:34). He had earned a reputation for being wise and kind, and in this situation, he persuaded the fuming leaders to settle down and choose a wiser response.

Gamaliel's principle follows advice from Scripture:

- "There is no wisdom, no insight, no plan that can succeed against the LORD" (Proverbs 21:30).
- "I make known the end from the beginning,
    from ancient times, what is still to come.
  I say, 'My purpose will stand,
    and I will do all that I please' " (Isaiah 46:10).
- "So if God gave them the same gift he gave us who believed in the Lord Jesus Christ, who was I to think that I could stand in God's way?" (Acts 11:17).

In the community of faith, there will be many opportunities to apply the "Gamaliel principle." You may deal with challenging relationships regularly, face and filter through new ideas, readjust unrealistic goals, or try out new methods. As you go forward, wisdom and power are given to you—just like it was given to the believers in Acts: "But they could not stand up against the wisdom the Spirit gave him as he spoke" (Acts 6:10).

INSIDE OUT

Read this passage in Acts, where Peter gains new insight into the church's ministry to the Gentiles:

While Peter was still speaking these words, the Holy Spirit came on all who heard the message. The circumcised believers who had come with Peter were astonished that the gift of the Holy Spirit had been poured out even on Gentiles. For they heard them speaking in tongues and praising God.

Then Peter said, "Surely no one can stand in the way of their being baptized with water. They have received the Holy Spirit just as we have" (Acts 10:44–47).

- When have you witnessed someone who is drenched with God's love and His power unmistakably?
- When you know that God's will and His plan will not be thwarted, does it compel you to participate or take a seat? Why?
- What was Peter's attitude toward the events in this story?
- Peter's confidence clearly came from God, but what specific experiences developed and strengthened his confidence?
- Consider the following texts:

    - Then Paul and Barnabas answered them boldly: "We had to speak the word of God to you first. Since you reject it and do not consider yourselves worthy of eternal life, we now turn to the Gentiles" (Acts 13:46).

    - So Paul and Barnabas spent considerable time there, speaking boldly for the Lord, who confirmed the message of his grace by enabling them to perform signs and wonders (Acts 14:3).

    - For two whole years Paul stayed there in his own rented house and welcomed all who came to see him. He proclaimed the kingdom of God and taught about the Lord Jesus Christ—with all boldness and without hindrance (Acts 28:30, 31).

22. DEACONATE

In those days when the number of disciples was increasing, the Hellenistic Jews among them complained against the Hebraic Jews because their widows were being overlooked in the daily distribution of food. So the Twelve gathered all the disciples together and said, "It would not be right for us to neglect the ministry of the word of God in order to wait on tables. Brothers and sisters, choose seven men from among you who are known to be full of the Spirit and wisdom. We will turn this responsibility over to them and will give our attention to prayer and the ministry of the word."

—Acts 6:1–4

Whenever you observe siblings who are required to share something, the exchange can be telling. For example, if two siblings have one cookie, it has to be divided thoughtfully and fairly. Most siblings watch to make sure it is divided equally. However, the eldest could argue that they need more calories. "It's more about biology than partiality," the older, bigger child might say.

In the budding community of the church, what became a handful grew to thousands.

Observe the growth:

- "In those days Peter stood up among the believers (a group numbering about a hundred and twenty)" (Acts 1:15).

- "Those who accepted his message were baptized, and about three thousand were added to their number that day" (Acts 2:41).
- "But many who heard the message believed; so the number of men who believed grew to about five thousand" (Acts 4:4).
- "Nevertheless, more and more men and women believed in the Lord and were added to their number" (Acts 5:14).

As a result of the growth, problems would naturally surface that leaders—such as Peter, James, and John—would be expected to handle. But the apostles were so overwhelmed by the whole task of this growing community that the best way to solve the problems that arose was to expand the leadership team.

Jesus once counseled His followers, "Therefore pray the Lord of the harvest to send out laborers into His harvest" (Matthew 9:38, NKJV). Sadly, many who are capable and ready to help are never called to take a post. Others have taken on a task or a cause where they felt that their contribution was helpful. At some point, the call to recruit more help must be given in order to solve problems or address emerging needs.

The complaint of the widows in Acts 6 is not a scandal or conspiracy. Rather it is the result of broken people who are seeking solutions to their problems. While you cannot dismiss the obvious tension between the Hebrews and the Hellenists, in the context of vibrant community, the unity should facilitate transcendence of the problem. Dismissing the problem can cause it to become a sore spot that can fester and grow.

You might remember two stories that are relevant to the issue of tensions between Jews and Gentiles:

- A woman who was Syro-Phoenician (Syrian and Greek) appealed to Jesus for her daughter to be healed from an evil spirit. The conversation went back and forth to teach a lesson to the disciples before ultimately arriving at the desired result—healing from oppression (see Matthew 15:21–28).
- In the story of the Roman centurion, the elders of the synagogue interceded for the centurion—even though he was a Gentile—because he was helpful, kind, and supported the Jewish cause. But the faith demonstrated by the centurion led Jesus to comment about him, "I tell you, I have not found such great faith even in Israel" (Luke 7:9).

Both stories capture the reality of racial tension and demonstrate steps toward becoming brothers and sisters in the faith. Denying the reality of racial tension—even in the church—only postpones the hard conversation for another day.

In this story in Acts, Peter led in the selection of a new set of leaders called deacons. Deacons were chosen according to three criteria: (1) they had to possess a *good reputation*, (2) they had to be full of *the Spirit*, and (3) they had to be full of *wisdom* (Acts 6:3). This story is a beautiful example of how Christian believers can overcome tensions and become more like Christ.

The impact of changing the leadership style from a "hero" to a "team" approach had an unmistakable effect, as observed at the end of the story, "So the word of God spread. The number of disciples in Jerusalem increased rapidly, and a large number of priests became obedient to the faith" (Acts 6:7).

Stephen was added to the group as part of the new team-leadership approach, and his performance of "great wonders and signs" (Acts 6:8) eventually incited some Jewish leaders (Saul of Tarsus among them) to silence his voice. However, before the enemies could silence Stephen's influence, there is a nuanced detail to the story we should examine.

Luke notes that "a large number of priests became obedient to the faith" (Acts 6:7). Out of all the groups opposing Jesus, the priests had the most to lose if Christianity gained a foothold. Sadducees could still play politics, the Pharisees and scribes could still ponder Scripture and theology, but the priests' world was the temple. The priesthood was a family tradition, and when Jesus brought an end to the need for the temple services by fulfilling His role as the Lamb of God, the priests were threatened most of all. Ironically, the religious leaders—who should have understood the nature of the sacrifice in the temple the most—responded negatively to the work of the Messiah.

What changed? Why did many priests join the followers of Christ? Maybe the dam finally broke—the evidence overwhelmed their barriers, and it was time. Maybe it was the beautiful scene of Jesus' hardworking hands bringing relief to widows and orphans. Maybe the reality of theology and practice unified together struck a resonating chord.

Regardless of exactly how and why people joined, the truth remains that people came to Jesus and found a place to belong and serve in the community.

INSIDE OUT

- Reflect on the people in your community that seem only to want to dismiss or tear down what you stand for. Why do you think they act that way?
- Are there parts of their story that you may not know about?
- Consider the following texts:
    - A person's wisdom yields patience; it is to one's glory to overlook an offense (Proverbs 19:11).
    - "But I tell you, love your enemies and pray for those who persecute you" (Matthew 5:44).
    - "A new command I give you: Love one another. As I have loved you, so you must love one another" (John 13:34).

23. CONCERNING STEPHEN

While they were stoning him, Stephen prayed, "Lord Jesus, receive my spirit." Then he fell on his knees and cried out, "Lord, do not hold this sin against them." When he had said this, he fell asleep.

—Acts 7:59, 60

Stephen was the first deacon to be chosen, along with six other leaders, to facilitate the growth of believers. The word *deacon* means "to serve" or "to be a minister." In Greek culture, the whole idea of serving others was undignified, even repugnant. Ruling over others was a proper occupation or station in life to aspire to. However, from the standpoint of a Jew, there was nothing embarrassing or disrespectful about working as a servant. From early childhood, they were expected to learn a trade or a skill. The process would be to "serve" and learn the trade and eventually teach someone younger those skills.

As the young church continued to grow, there was a need to develop new leaders that would function in accordance with the needs of the community. It is important to understand that all of the believers would embrace being servants for the cause of the kingdom of God. Jesus said to the disciples, "Whoever wants to become great among you must be your servant" (Matthew 20:26).

When Stephen was called to function as a deacon, the job involved serving in the more practical matters of life. It is true that deacons were chosen to wait on tables, so to speak, but it becomes clear that there was more involved. The basic operations of a deacon include benevolence, financial matters, logistics, and serving the overall needs of the church and the community. This is "the cornbread and beans" of everyday life in the church.

Job descriptions for leaders in the early church can be compiled by attending to the subtleties and direct charges in Scripture. It was noted about the first deacon, "Now Stephen, a man full of God's grace and power, performed great wonders and signs among the people" (Acts 6:8). "Waiting on tables" does not correspond to that description. If you think that Stephen was just a waiter for the church, keep reading.

There are two full chapters in the book of Acts about Stephen's ministry. Whether it was a compliment or not, the enemies of the gospel were hyperfocused on trying to get rid of Stephen. Of all the characters in the gospels and at the beginning of the new church, Stephen steps out of the shadows and has an immediate impact on the work of Christ.

The record describes Stephen's reputation as being "a man full of God's grace and power, [who] performed great wonders and signs among the people" (Acts 6:8). Furthermore, those critics who came to intimidate Stephen personally discovered that this deacon confounded them with the wisdom and the power of the Holy Spirit (Acts 6:9, 10).

It became clear that Stephen was a formidable and fearless preacher of the gospel of Christ. If you read Acts 6 in its entirety, you'll see that the chapter finishes with the uncompromising pride of the Jewish leaders and the unconquerable conviction of Stephen. It was noted that the people could see God's glory when he spoke: "His face was like the face of an angel" (Acts 6:15).

At the stoning of Stephen, two undeniable memories seared into the minds of the witnesses that day: Even though the rocks fell on Stephen, he only saw the vision of his Savior and shouted, "Look, . . . I see heaven open and the Son of Man standing at the right hand of God" (Acts 7:56). And as Stephen was dying, he was pleading for God to forgive his killers. One person would eventually appreciate his words of forgiveness—Saul of Tarsus would one day accept the forgiveness Jesus freely offers to all who receive His gift of salvation.

The persecutors of Christ thought that death would snuff out the fire for this revolution, but they were wrong. Those who witnessed Stephen's death realized the truth of Jesus' life, death, and resurrection anew.

INSIDE OUT

Think about the story of Paul in connection with the stoning of Stephen. Jesus once prophesied that one day people would persecute believers thinking they were helping God's cause:

> "All this I have told you so that you will not fall away. They will put you out of the synagogue; in fact, the time is coming when anyone who kills you will think they are offering a service to God. . . .
>
> ". . . A time is coming and in fact has come when you will be scattered, each to your own home. You will leave me all alone. Yet

I am not alone, for my Father is with me.

"I have told you these things, so that in me you may have peace. In this world you will have trouble. But take heart! I have overcome the world" (John 16:1, 2, 32, 33).

- What are the differences between the community Paul wrote to the Corinthians (1 Corinthians 12) about and the community that stoned Stephen?
- What were the different motivating factors between those two separate times in Paul's life?
- Consider the following texts:

  - What is more, I consider everything a loss because of the surpassing worth of knowing Christ Jesus my Lord, for whose sake I have lost all things. I consider them garbage, that I may gain Christ (Philippians 3:8).

  - "Death has been swallowed up in victory. Where, O death, is your victory? Where, O death, is your sting?" (1 Corinthians 15:54, 55).

24. DIVINE APPOINTMENTS

The Spirit told Philip,
"Go to that chariot and stay near it."
Then Philip ran up to the chariot
and heard the man reading Isaiah
the prophet. "Do you understand
what you are reading?" Philip asked.
"How can I," he said, "unless someone
explains it to me?" *So he invited*
Philip to come up and sit with him.
—*Acts 8:29–31; emphasis added*

A quick look through the book of Acts shows the miraculous on every page. "Wonders and signs" (Acts 6:8) pop up in nearly every story. The words of an apostle awaken the dead. Angels show up and pick the locks of prison doors. A rushing wind comes with fire and—boom!—the language barriers are gone. Your weekly routines might seem mind-numbing compared to life in the early church!

In the ancient world, the supernatural and the natural world were separated by a thin curtain. There were no coincidences or random "lucky" moments. For sure, if something significant happened, it occurred by the hand of God or other forces. But today, knowledge claims a level of sophistication that often kills the sense of wonder.

If a friend tells you today, "I heard a voice speaking to me last night," what would you say? You would probably go through the rational checkpoints in your mind because, in a modern era, there are other explanations for what appears to be supernatural.

As you read this story in Acts 8, orient your mind and prepare for another story filled with wonder. In the normal, humdrum routine of the new church, an angel of the Lord shows up and speaks to Philip, saying, "Go south to the road—the desert road—that goes down from Jerusalem to Gaza" (Acts 8:26).

In that time, other religions had lost their hold on the hearts of people. Maybe those who followed pagan gods felt tired from meeting the demands of devotion. For those who were searching for a god in favor of human decency, they found a refreshing truth in putting their faith in Jehovah. The constant drive of selfish ambitions has a way of subsiding once you learn that you were created "in the image of God" (Genesis 1:27).

The voice that urged Philip to go south set him on the same road as a chariot-riding traveler. The occupant was struggling with a passage of Scripture. Who was this man? Where was he going? What was he doing? Here are some answers:

- The man was a high-ranking officer in the court of Candace, queen of Ethiopia.
- The man was southbound on his way home after worshiping in Jerusalem.
- The man was reading Isaiah from a scroll, specifically the prophecy of the Messiah's suffering and sacrifice.

In humility, the man was searching for help to understand the passage that says:

> He was oppressed and afflicted,
> yet he did not open his mouth;
> he was led like a lamb to the slaughter,
> and as a sheep before its shearers is silent,
> so he did not open his mouth.
> By oppression and judgment he was taken away.
> Yet who of his generation protested?
> For he was cut off from the land of the living;
> for the transgression of my people he was punished (Isaiah 53:7, 8).

The story of the Ethiopian is a reminder that many are searching for God. It is still true that you are not made to be alone and that you need to walk with others on the journey. This story stirs up many thoughts about community, but the truth emerges that there is a hidden work going inside of all.

If you haven't yet noticed, the early church was active because the Holy Spirit is active! When the Holy Spirit prompts a believer to be available for anything, those who are ready end up in the center of the action.

- If it is food for the hungry, God will provide—be ready, be there.
- If someone is sick and needs healing, God will provide—be ready, be there.
- If someone has a broken heart and needs a friend, God will provide—be ready, be there.
- If a seeker needs a Bible study, God will provide everything you need to answer their questions—be ready, be there.

Bible study is not complicated. Simply sharing what you see in and know from Scripture with someone is the most basic, salient moment of Christian service. Trust God to put you on the road to Gaza—or another road that you don't know just yet.

- "But the Advocate, the Holy Spirit, whom the Father will send in my name, will teach you all things and will remind you of everything I have said to you" (John 14:26).
- "Do not worry about how you will defend yourselves or what you will say, for the Holy Spirit will teach you at that time what you should say" (Luke 12:11, 12).
- "Then Philip began with that very passage of Scripture and told him the good news about Jesus" (Acts 8:35).

The results shouldn't be a surprise. The CFO of Ethiopia requested baptism; before they had even dried off, Philip was transported by the Holy Spirit to another district. Amazing!

INSIDE OUT

- If you were to pray for a divine appointment, how would you recognize it when it came?
- Looking back, do you see evidence that this kind of guidance has influenced you already?
- How can you take the initiative in speaking about what God has done for you this week?
- Consider the following texts:

  On arriving there, they gathered the church together and reported all that God had done through them and how he had opened a door of faith to the Gentiles (Acts 14:27).

  Paul greeted them and reported in detail what God had done among the Gentiles through his ministry (Acts 21:19).

  I will not venture to speak of anything except what Christ has accomplished through me in leading the Gentiles to obey God by what I have said and done (Romans 15:18).

25. BEFORE AND AFTER

Then Ananias went to the house and entered it. Placing his hands on Saul, he said, "Brother Saul, the Lord—Jesus, who appeared to you on the road as you were coming here—has sent me so that you may see again and be filled with the Holy Spirit." Immediately, something like scales fell from Saul's eyes, and he could see again. He got up and was baptized, and after taking some food, he regained his strength.

—Acts 9:17–19

Before-and-after pictures are used to sell a product or process that the vendor claims will produce a visible improvement. The before-and-after pictures of weight-loss programs show obvious changes in weight, better muscle mass and tone, improved skin, shinier hair, and nicer clothing. Other images feature the changes made by a car restoration or a kitchen remodel or the difference in students' scores after employing a new teaching methodology.

Think about before-and-after images. How much of the real difference is made just by a change of expression on the person's face? The before pictures show a stale stare, while the after images shows a smiling countenance. The message is immediate: "You will be happier when you experience the difference for yourself."

The before-and-after pictures of Saul turned into Paul were remarkable. Imagine this before picture: "Meanwhile, Saul was still breathing out murderous threats against the Lord's disciples" (Acts 9:1). Apparently, the persecutor was visibly passionate about his crusade. When the stoning of Stephen occurred, the persecutor was present, and the Bibles notes, "Saul approved of their killing him" (Acts 8:1).

Consider the moment Saul saw the light on the road to Damascus:

> Suddenly a light from heaven flashed around him. He fell to the ground and heard a voice say to him, "Saul, Saul, why do you persecute me?"
>
> "Who are you, Lord?" Saul asked.
>
> "I am Jesus, whom you are persecuting," he replied. "Now get up and go into the city, and you will be told what you must do" (Acts 9:3–6).

The story resolves in a living room in Damascus, where Paul sat blind and praying. After three days, Paul heard Ananias speak words that he would never forget: "Brother Saul, the Lord—Jesus, who appeared to you on the road as you were coming here—has sent me so that you may see again and be filled with the Holy Spirit" (Acts 9:17).

Now visualize the after image. The dynamic story produces a perfect before-and-after picture of transformation. Saul believed in God with devotion and unquestionable commitment. In his zeal for the kingdom of God, he had missed a few facts along the way, but once he grasped the truth about Jesus, the change was impressive!

What changed? His view of Jesus. The stories he memorized as a child of Moses, Elijah, Esther, and Daniel were still the same. But when someone moves from hating Jesus to believing in Jesus, that change causes a significant shift in a person's life.

What didn't change? Paul was still zealous, passionate, and single-minded. Read what he penned about his mission statement to the believers in Philippi:

> Watch out for those dogs, those evildoers, those mutilators of the flesh. . . .
>
> If someone else thinks they have reasons to put confidence in the flesh, I have more: circumcised on the eighth day, of the people of Israel, of the tribe of Benjamin, a Hebrew of Hebrews; in regard to the law, a Pharisee; as for zeal, persecuting the church; as for righteousness based on the law, faultless.
>
> But whatever were gains to me I now consider loss for the sake of Christ. What is more, I consider everything a loss because of the surpassing worth of knowing Christ Jesus my Lord, for whose sake I have lost all things (Philippians 3:2, 4–8).

This passage reveals that Paul is intense.

To his little brother in Christ, he proclaimed, "Here is a trustworthy saying that deserves full acceptance: Christ Jesus came into the world to save sinners—of whom *I am the worst*" (1 Timothy 1:15; emphasis added). Would you consider Paul high-maintenance or a glory seeker? No. Paul was not proud of having played a role in the death of Stephen, one of the beloved leaders in Christ's church. Knowing there needed to be serious adjustments in his worldview, Paul explained, "My immediate response was not to consult any human being. I did not go up to Jerusalem to see those who were apostles before I was, but I went into Arabia. Later I returned to Damascus" (Galatians 1:16, 17).

When you look at your journey, do you see before-and-after changes in yourself? You may struggle with the fact that nothing much seems to have changed at all. You see transformation in others, but it is so difficult to see growth in yourself. There may be "Damascus road" moments where you "saw the light" and then there are the three-year retreats where the adjustments in your mind take time.

INSIDE OUT

- Has something like Paul's experience on the Damascus road happened to you?
- Has there been a time when you were headed in one direction, and then God turned you in the opposite direction?
- Consider the following texts:

  - Do not conform to the pattern of this world, but be transformed by the renewing of your mind. Then you will be able to test and approve what God's will is—his good, pleasing and perfect will (Romans 12:2).

  - Therefore, if anyone is in Christ, the new creation has come: The old has gone, the new is here (2 Corinthians 5:17).

  - I have been crucified with Christ and I no longer live, but Christ lives in me. The life I now live in the body, I live by faith in the Son of God, who loved me and gave himself for me (Galatians 2:20).

26. TABITHA'S LEGACY

In Joppa there was a disciple named Tabitha (in Greek her name is Dorcas); she was always doing good and helping the poor. About that time she became sick and died, and her body was washed and placed in an upstairs room.
—Acts 9:36, 37

- Police officer
- Firefighter
- Nurse
- Military officer
- Housekeeper
- Chef
- Pilot
- Fast-food employee
- Doctor
- Lifeguard

All of the preceding occupations require uniforms. In addition, many schools have adopted a uniform policy. Most of the people who wear uniforms would rather not. If you search on the internet for "Adventist Dorcas Society" and scan through the images, you will recognize the uniforms they wear in the African chapter—bright blue skirts with a stark-white blouse. You may recognize them by their uniform, but you will know them by their service to people.

The Dorcas Society was named after a woman in the Bible named Tabitha. Before the story starts, the text describes her work, stating, "She was always doing good and helping the poor" (Acts 9:36).

After such a noble introduction, you might expect a stirring story about her kindness to others. But after telling the readers that she had been an amazing worker for good, the next phrase announces that Dorcas got sick and died.

It doesn't matter if you are young or old when someone dies, there is an inner voice that cries out in protest. Deep down, we know that we were created to live forever, but sin has separated us from the life God originally intended for us. In this case, the believers in Joppa could not accept the death of Tabitha and sent for Peter to pray for a miracle.

The request for Tabitha to be raised from death was never articulated. The believers' message simply asked Peter to come. So Peter came. Everyone gathered in the room where Tabitha's body lay and held articles of clothing that she had made for them. Quite simply, they knew that God could raise the dead, and they believed He would raise Tabitha back to life. The community showed up to grieve Tabitha's death.

Peter sent the crowd outside, "then he got down on his knees and prayed. Turning toward the dead woman, he said, 'Tabitha, get up' " (Acts 9:40). And she did! Then Peter "took her by the hand and helped her to her feet. Then he called for the believers, especially the widows, and presented her to them alive" (Acts 9:41).

The record of Scripture tells of miracles and wonders as a way of life in the church. Tabitha's life of ministry combined with her resurrection was more than a miracle; it started a revolution of goodness that has continued for centuries.

Two thousand years later, women wear a blue-and-white uniform and carry bags full of clothes and food for widows. They are a part of the Dorcas Society in an African country. Sometimes they bring clothes, food, medicine, blankets, repaired tools, charcoal, backpacks, school supplies, or even flowers. They teach young mothers how to to be healthy, faithful, and kind to others in their community. These women carry on Tabitha's legacy.

Who do you know that reminds you of Tabitha?

INSIDE OUT

- James 1:27 defines pure religion as good deeds. How can pure religion become your lifestyle like it was for Tabitha?
- Consider the following texts:

    - Religion that God our Father accepts as pure and faultless is this: to look after orphans and widows in their distress and to keep oneself from being polluted by the world (James 1:27).

    - What good is it, my brothers and sisters, if someone claims to have faith but has no deeds? Can such faith save them? Suppose a brother or a sister is without clothes and daily food. If one of you says to them, "Go in peace; keep warm and well fed," but does nothing about their physical needs, what good is it? In the same way, faith by itself, if it is not accompanied by action, is dead.

But someone will say, "You have faith; I have deeds."

Show me your faith without deeds, and I will show you my faith by my deeds (James 2:14–18).

He will put the sheep on his right and the goats on his left.

Then the King will say to those on his right, "Come, you who are blessed by my Father; take your inheritance, the kingdom prepared for you since the creation of the world. For I was hungry and you gave me something to eat, I was thirsty and you gave me something to drink, I was a stranger and you invited me in, I needed clothes and you clothed me, I was sick and you looked after me, I was in prison and you came to visit me" (Matthew 25:33–36).

27. ONE DREAM

Then Peter began to speak: "I now realize how true it is that God does not show favoritism but accepts from every nation the one who fears him and does what is right."
—Acts 10:34, 35

When have you experienced partiality, either in your favor or in favor of someone else? Have you been given an opportunity because of someone you knew? Is it possible that people perceive your character and contribution in light of your background—for good or bad? The book of Acts records a growing problem in the Christian church centered on relations between Jews and Gentiles.

For a Jew to be versed and trained in the Scriptures, they would know that their nation originated from one family. The same family would also see the seed of Abraham's family give birth to the Messiah, the Son of God. However, it is also true that the mission of Abraham's family is to attract and invite people into God's family.

If you see favoritism, racism, and preferred status in the world around you and are frustrated by the degree to which these mind-sets are so ingrained, you are not alone. Remember when Jesus charged into the temple to make a "clean sweep" of things that were wrong? The temple officials had implemented requirements for sacrifices that cost the average person dearly.

Jesus saw these expenses—the outrageous human-made impediments that were designed to keep all but the privileged from coming close to the altar of forgiveness—and He had had enough! His words echoed a truth that comes from long ago as He delivered the reprimand: "Is it not written: 'My house will be called a house of prayer for all nations'? But you have made it 'a den of robbers' " (Mark 11:17). Jesus looked upon the one place where God's face should shine mercy, redemption, grace, and restoration to sincere seekers, but God's face was obscured through the requirements and expenses the religious leaders had instigated. Jesus reminded the people of the prophet's words, "My house will be called a house of prayer for all nations" (Mark 11:17).

God started the work of reconciliation long ago. Some seasons bore more and better fruit in this regard than others, but His work of repentance and restoration has persevered throughout history. The Day of Pentecost was a serious opportunity for a season of reconciliation between God and humanity, Jew and Gentile. Then when Peter recounted his vision, his message, and his own conviction as a follower of Christ in Acts 10, the season of change was timely. The barrier between Jew and Gentile was being torn down.

If you sometimes feel discouraged about the divisions in the community of faith, return to Acts 10 and remember that God is in the business of reconciling people—to Him and to each other. In this story of the community of faith in Acts 10, they made things right over time. It started with two people—Cornelius and Peter—sharing the same dream for the community of Christ.

INSIDE OUT

- Here are three passages that apply to this chapter. They have the same theme but specifically different reasons. What are the differences between the three in practice and theory?
    - But now apart from the law the righteousness of God has been made known, to which the Law and the Prophets testify. This righteousness is given through faith in Jesus Christ to all who believe (Romans 3:21, 22).
    - For we were all baptized by one Spirit so as to form one body—whether Jews or Gentiles, slave or free—and we were all given the one Spirit to drink (1 Corinthians 12:13).
    - So in Christ Jesus you are all children of God through faith, for all of you who were baptized into Christ have clothed yourselves with Christ. There is neither Jew nor Gentile, neither slave nor free, nor is there male and female, for you are all one in Christ Jesus (Galatians 3:26–28).

28. LOVE ONE ANOTHER

"A new command I give you: Love one another. As I have loved you, so you must love one another. By this everyone will know that you are my disciples, if you love one another."
—John 13:34, 35; emphasis added

Imagine you are a child opening your first present on Christmas morning. As the paper falls away, your face displays surprise, which becomes confusion, "What am I seeing?" You look toward your mother, at first bewildered, then disappointed. "Is this a joke?"

She stares at you with unfazed glee. "Do you like it?"

Maybe you look to your father for clarity, but he is fully engaged in putting batteries into a new gadget for Uncle Joe.

Before you is the same toy you received last year for Christmas. It's not a newer version; it is the *same* toy. Familiar scratches and spots of rubbed-off paint mark the item. Your parents packaged up your old toy and put it under the tree for you again this year. *What is this?*

While this scenario could result in disappointment, it's true that we do repurpose or resell items that we own from time to time. When people want to sell old or used items, they might be labeled as

- a classic car,
- a reconditioned tool,
- a refurbished computer,
- a gently used toy, or
- vintage clothes.

It is fine to buy old or used items that are a good deal, but when you sell them, please don't package them as "new." Yet, when Jesus announces, "A new commandment I give to you, that you love one another" (John 13:34, NKJV), how do you respond? "Love each other" is not a new idea; it's an old commandment. It's almost like your parent handed you an old toy wrapped in new packaging and said, "Surprise!"

Loving others is an old command. Leviticus 19:18 reads, "Do not seek revenge or bear a grudge against anyone among your people, but love your neighbor as yourself. I am the LORD." However, it makes more sense if the word "new" doesn't necessarily mean "brand-new" but refers to a refreshed, restored item to revalue for its timeless—and perhaps priceless—qualities.

Why do we need another "new" commandment to love others? The word "love" is overused. You can love chocolate, cats, snow, old cars, smoothies, shoes, soccer, and your spouse. But Jesus provided us with a new *example* of love, a way to flesh out the original concept in order to increase our understanding and appreciation. Also, Jesus' new commandment to love others will *distinguish* you as His disciple.

Jesus' life provides an example of what He means when He commanded His followers to love each other:

- "Love one another." A new commandment has a new example—a new model for you to compare to the old. When Jesus washed the disciples' feet, they witnessed a "new" example of love: "I have set you an example that you should do as I have done for you" (John 13:15). To make sure that they got the point, Jesus reviewed the lesson, asking, "Do you understand what I have done for you?" (John 13:12). Later, He clarified it again by saying, "My command is this: Love each other as I have loved you. Greater love has no one than this: to lay down one's life for one's friends" (John 15:12, 13).
- "Love one another" is a new commandment that will have distinguishing qualities. "Greater love" has no competition in life. The first and best attribute of God's character is laying down His life for humanity. The action has no equal. God is never going to appear more vividly than that.

Your love for others will define you. In a world of fakes, myths, and hoaxes, disciples of Christ are defined by one essential mark—they love one another. When He became flesh and walked with humanity, people could see the character of God in the person of Christ. You can recognize, share, and experience the Father's kingdom on earth as your love for others becomes obvious. Truly, "no one has ever seen God; but if we love one another, God lives in us and his love is made complete in us" (1 John 4:12).

When Jesus calls the community of faith, He brings

- a new teaching (Mark 1:27; Acts 17:19),
- a new wine and new wineskins (Luke 5:37–39),
- a new command (John 13:34; 1 John 2:7, 8; 2 John 5),
- a new covenant (Luke 22:20; 1 Corinthians 11:25; 2 Corinthians 3:6),
- a new creation (2 Corinthians 5:17; Galatians 6:15),

- a new self (Ephesians 2:15; 4:24; Colossians 3:10),
- a new heaven and earth (2 Peter 3:13; Revelation 21:1),
- a new name (Revelation 2:17; 3:12),
- a new Jerusalem (Revelation 3:12; 21:2),
- a new song (Revelation 5:9; 14:3), and
- an all-things-new reality (Revelation 21:5).

INSIDE OUT

- Consider the "new commandment" that Jesus charged His disciples to obey. What is the command? What is new about the new rule? Why should we follow it?
- What does it look like to love like Christ?
- What difference would it make if we loved this way? What difference would it make if we disobeyed this command?
- Consider the following texts:
    - And this is his command: to believe in the name of his Son, Jesus Christ, and to love one another as he commanded us (1 John 3:23).
    - The one who keeps God's commands lives in him, and he in them. And this is how we know that he lives in us: We know it by the Spirit he gave us (1 John 3:24).
    - Not only so, but we also glory in our sufferings, because we know that suffering produces perseverance; perseverance, character; and character, hope. And hope does not put us to shame, because God's love has been poured out into our hearts through the Holy Spirit, who has been given to us (Romans 5:3–5).

29. LIKE-MINDED WITH ONE ANOTHER

Live in harmony with one another. Do not be proud, but be willing to associate with people of low position. Do not be conceited.

—Romans 12:16

How do you process information as a learner? Do you favor visual information? Or perhaps you are more kinesthetic in your learning style? If you are an auditory learner, you will process information more easily through listening. While you may use all of the modes of learning, there is usually a predominant style.

In the New Testament, the experience of the church community displayed a like-minded purpose. It is clear that people were very different, yet shared life experiences uniquely shape the group, like a fingerprint or a DNA sequence is unique. When the two or three or ten, show up to "do life" in community, the work of becoming like-minded is necessary. This means that in order to thrive, members must recognize the differences but also the values common to the group. Whether it is a group project, task, or shared experience, everyone values the priority of the common part over the unique nuances of the individual.

The state of like-mindedness requires mixing with others in the community. In the church community, this may look like the following:

- Gathering for worship
- Conducting a small-group Bible study
- Going on a mission trip to El Salvador
- Making strategic plans for sharing the gospel

The New Testament has many exhortations for individual believers who spend intentional time with the body of believers. Following are a few of them:

- "Finally, all of you, be like-minded, be sympathetic, love one another, be compassionate and humble" (1 Peter 3:8).
- "Therefore if you have any encouragement from being united with Christ, if any comfort from his love, if any common sharing in the

Spirit, if any tenderness and compassion, then make my joy complete by being like-minded, having the same love, being one in spirit and of one mind" (Philippians 2:1, 2).
- "May the God who gives endurance and encouragement give you the same attitude of mind toward each other that Christ Jesus had" (Romans 15:5).

Surveying Scripture and the memories of your experience, you know how crucial like-mindedness is for us to understand. The enemy of *harmony* is the word *haughty*, or looking down on others. The dirty little secret we humans carry is thinking more highly of our own preferences, and we let those of others fall lower on the scale. To say that it's unavoidable does not mean that we shouldn't work on mixing or adjust our mind-set to be "like-minded."

You might see this propensity for haughtiness when people share their ideas, opinions, and perceptions. Debates on the news, in politics, and in town-hall sessions are fertile ground for dissension rather than like-mindedness. When you observe people involved in these things, note how many are not listening well to others. They might use words or phrases that show that they are hearing the other person, but are they listening to try to understand? Rarely. Winning the argument is the goal and the prize, and the haughty attitude is unmistakable.

The hard work of mixing well in the community of faith comes when a member believes they share the same basic principles with the community, even though unique perspectives are also present. With that view, like-mindedness can grow. If you play nice with your words but think naughty in your mind, the discord will rise to the surface eventually.

The struggle in the new church centered on how people functioned with one another. In stories where favoritism is responded to by Spirit-guided leaders who value like-mindedness, the result is growth. In the pivotal moments between Jews and Gentiles, the hard work of harmony found the best result, which is being Christian.

Today, you will find opportunities to mix well with others. As you practice your "one another" mind-set, may your hard-but-good work be fruitful.

INSIDE OUT

- What are some areas in your community in which you think you are all "like-minded"?
- What are some areas that cause dissonance within your community?
- What changes can God make in your attitude toward others that can bridge the gap between those points of dissonance?
- Consider the following texts:
    - For by the grace given me I say to every one of you: Do not think of

yourself more highly than you ought, but rather think of yourself with sober judgment, in accordance with the faith God has distributed to each of you (Romans 12:3).

- By the grace God has given me, I laid a foundation as a wise builder, and someone else is building on it. But each one should build with care (1 Corinthians 3:10).
- For who makes you different from anyone else? What do you have that you did not receive? And if you did receive it, why do you boast as though you did not? (1 Corinthians 4:7).

30. ACCEPT ONE ANOTHER

Accept one another, then, just as Christ accepted you, in order to bring praise to God.
—Romans 15:7

When you click the Accept button on the terms and conditions for your technology, do you truly know what you are accepting? When you ask a young person, "Do you know what it means when you click the Accept button?" they will reply quickly, saying, "It means that I can play the game now."

If you read all of the fine print on every page of an agreement, it's probably because it's your job to know it. The rest of the world clicks Accept because there are certain rules, laws, and liabilities that you assume are in alignment with your worldview. Hopefully, that is true.

Acceptance is more complicated than you might think. How many times have you asked for forgiveness in prayer and believed it? Surely, God has heard this petition before. The difficult step is not asking for acceptance, but believing that God will actually extend it. You don't need to be an ax murderer or serial liar to struggle with accepting God's forgiveness. Paul struggled with guilt because what he had done sickened him. Digging deeper into your own heart is painful work, as Paul admits:

> For I know that good itself does not dwell in me, that is, in my sinful nature. For I have the desire to do what is good, but I cannot carry it out. For I do not do the good I want to do, but the evil I do not want to do—this I keep on doing. . . .
>
> What a wretched man I am! Who will rescue me from this body that is subject to death? Thanks be to God, who delivers me through Jesus Christ our Lord!
>
> So then, I myself in my mind am a slave to God's law, but in my sinful nature a slave to the law of sin (Romans 7:18, 19, 24, 25).

Accepting God's amazing, almost unbelievable gift is the only option for salvation. You can pay for yourself, or you can let Someone pay for you. Your cost? "For the wages of sin is death" (Romans 6:23). Or you can let

Someone pay for you: "But the *gift* of God is eternal life in Christ Jesus our Lord" (Romans 6:23; emphasis added).

You see, accepting is more involved than agreeing to the message of a clever meme or spiritual slogan on a T-shirt. Again, Paul explains:

"You see, at just the right time, when we were still powerless, Christ died for the ungodly. Very rarely will anyone die for a righteous person, though for a good person someone might possibly dare to die. But God demonstrates his own love for us in this: While we were still sinners, Christ died for us" (Romans 5:6–8).

When you hug someone, usually, the acceptance of the embrace is simultaneous with the action. Sometimes you experience awkward moments where the nature of the relationship is uncertain. Do you reach out for a hug or a handshake? What happens when you reach out your hand for a handshake, but they say, "Bring it in!"

Have you embraced someone who did not return the embrace? To not accept is to reject. Acceptance requires complete investment in a relationship or an idea. Accepting others takes practice in order to develop the easy embrace, but the awkward moments last for only a short time.

Consider the trust fall as an illustration of learning about accepting one another. Watching the trepidation and visible conflict of those who fall from a platform into the arms of a handful of people is beautiful. You see, those who make the plunge fall with their own style: screaming, crying, flailing, buckling, kicking, sitting, and some saying words that you should avoid. Some fall with easy grace, but they still fall. The commitment to accept the embrace is awkward, but it is complete.

After the Resurrection, the church experienced signs and wonders that created a sense of unique euphoria. But after a while, more unbelievable events occurred when people—Jews and Gentiles—entered into an embrace that filled the world with awe.

How did they learn to accept one another? As in the trust fall example, they fell. However, the real reason had to do with an example set by Christ: "Accept one another, then, *just as Christ accepted you*" (Romans 15:7; emphasis added).

The path to accepting others starts with knowing God's acceptance in your own heart. Accepting is not simply not rejecting or tolerating another person; it's welcoming them into an embrace—embracing that Christ has fully accepted you.

Today's culture promotes the catchphrase of "acceptance," but the deeper and more enduring experience is found in surrendering to God's love. This experience forces us all to admit brokenness and fall, easily or awkwardly, into the embrace of God's grace.

INSIDE OUT

- What events from your past make it hard for you to believe God accepts you?
- Why do you think people are more likely to change after, rather than before, they find acceptance?
- Some churches go so far in accepting others that they accept those who are living in open sin (see 1 Corinthians 5:9–13). Where is the balance between accepting sinners yet not accepting their sin?
- Why is it important to keep God's grace rather than our happiness as our primary aim in our relationships?
- Consider the following texts:

    - Whoever pursues righteousness and love finds life, prosperity and honor (Proverbs 21:21).

    - This righteousness is given through faith in Jesus Christ to all who believe. There is no difference between Jew and Gentile, for all have sinned and fall short of the glory of God, and all are justified freely by his grace through the redemption that came by Christ Jesus (Romans 3:22–24).

    - The Lord is not slow in keeping his promise, as some understand slowness. Instead he is patient with you, not wanting anyone to perish, but everyone to come to repentance (2 Peter 3:9).

31. SERVE

You, my brothers and sisters, were called to be free. But do not use your freedom to indulge the flesh; rather serve one another *humbly in love.*
—Galatians 5:13; emphasis added

Have you ever forgotten your keys, wallet, PIN, or passwords? Do you remember to send thank-you cards? Or feed the pet fish? Remembering what you sometimes forget is frustrating because most people don't plan to forget things.

Then there are things you will never forget—but wish you could—such as kidney stones, root canals, or food poisoning. Even more painful than physical suffering is the trauma of emotional pain—being caught in a lie, the shame of asking for financial assistance, disappointing your loved ones, or feeling the pain of betrayal. Sometimes there are experiences in life that are so painful you just want to block them out.

Your memory is one of the most complicated functions of the brain, and it is the epicenter for making decisions. It's one of the body's involuntary functions, yet remembering and forgetting are keys to understanding sin and salvation.

In Galatians 5:13, Paul calls us all to "serve one another," but this statement comes in the middle of a conversation about remembering the experience of the slavery of sin. He warns: "Do not let yourselves be burdened again by a yoke of slavery" (Galatians 5:1). Notice the paradox of God's kingdom—when you escape slavery, you are called to "serve one another." The word "serve" could mean "to be a slave," which might seem like a contradiction, but consider Jesus' words about submitting to a different yoke on your shoulders. You might remember a similar paradox when Jesus called, "Come to me, all you who are weary and burdened, and I will give you rest. Take my yoke upon you and learn from me, for I am gentle and humble in heart, and you will find rest for your souls. For my yoke is easy and my burden is light" (Matthew 11:28–30).

In every paradox, there is a statement that seems to be a contradiction, but after more thought, the initial idea becomes profoundly clear. Take a walk down memory lane:

- "Remember that you were slaves in Egypt and the LORD your God redeemed you from there. That is why I command you to do this" (Deuteronomy 24:18).
- "Do not mistreat or oppress a foreigner, for you were foreigners in Egypt" (Exodus 22:21).
- "The foreigner residing among you must be treated as your native-born. Love them as yourself, for you were foreigners in Egypt. I am the LORD your God" (Leviticus 19:34).
- "Do not despise an Edomite, for the Edomites are related to you. Do not despise an Egyptian, because you resided as foreigners in their country" (Deuteronomy 23:7).
- "Remember that you were slaves in Egypt. That is why I command you to do this" (Deuteronomy 24:22).

How do you avoid exiting from one type of slavery and entering into another? Choose to serve, and you'll live above the oppression. If slavery is all around you, take the power of oppression away by choosing to live above it.

Consider the people in your life that love to serve others. When they choose to help others, does it seem like they drag a ball and chain on their leg? When you imagine yourself doing the most noble, virtuous, and Christlike endeavor that you can think of, you likely imagine yourself doing something selfless. In another letter, Paul offers an invitation to the community of faith:

> In your relationships with one another, have the same mindset as Christ Jesus:
>
> Who, being in very nature God,
>   did not consider equality with God
> something to be used to his own advantage;
> rather, he made himself nothing
>   by taking the very nature of a servant,
>   being made in human likeness.
> And being found in appearance as a man,
>   he humbled himself
>   by becoming obedient to death—
>   even death on a cross (Philippians 2:5–8).

In Jesus' day, the law allowed a Roman soldier to command a Jew to carry his pack for up to a mile. By doing so, the Jews were reminded of the authority and power of Rome. However, Jesus told His followers to carry the pack a second mile voluntarily.

The state of being truly free does not come from a physical uprising or a revolution but from voluntarily serving others who are in authority, showing that God's power is greater than slavery. The kingdom of Rome operated from power and conquest, but the kingdom of Christ finds its power through serving people one at a time. Choosing the radical love of serving others will transcend the power of force.

In life, the first mile is expected and demanded—the second mile is a gift. When you go the second mile, it causes the world to wonder, *Why?* When you go the second mile, the nature of conversation changes from superficial to meaningful. When you go the second mile, you show there is more than this life. When you go the second mile, it proves there is a power greater than this world. When you go the second mile, you demonstrate there is a greater love that only comes from giving more than is expected of you.

As you walk in a world where the expectations for helping others are relatively low, serving others is one way to remind yourself that you were set free.

INSIDE OUT

- Think of ways that you can apply Christian service to your spheres of influence this next week. What would the impact be if you made a habit of this?
- When you witness someone else practice the "extra mile" lifestyle, how does it affect you?
- What are the ways that you can encourage the attitude of service in others throughout this week?
- Consider the following texts:

    - "You are the salt of the earth. But if the salt loses its saltiness, how can it be made salty again? It is no longer good for anything, except to be thrown out and trampled underfoot" (Matthew 5:13).

    - You, my brothers and sisters, were called to be free. But do not use your freedom to indulge the flesh; rather, serve one another humbly in love (Galatians 5:13).

    - Though I am free and belong to no one, I have made myself a slave to everyone, to win as many as possible (1 Corinthians 9:19).

32. BEAR ANOTHER'S BURDEN

Carry each other's burdens, *and in this way you will fulfill the law of Christ.*
—Galatians 6:2; emphasis added

There are reasons you should never go backpacking alone—safety is an obvious consideration, and possible boredom is another. If there is an accident, one is going to do the suffering part while the other person does the panic part of the experience. No backpacking story is interesting to the listener unless there is some pain and hysteria mixed in with awe-inspiring photography. I recommend always backpacking with a friend for safety and a sense of community.

Another point to consider is the value of sharing the load when you are backpacking. If two people are backpacking in the wilderness and they are sharing a tent, who packs the extra weight? The average weight of a decent tent for two is about five pounds. If each of you were to carry a single-person tent (three and a half pounds), you would shoulder more weight in the end than you would by sharing the load. Especially since you are going to walk with a pack already, make it easier and share the load! When Paul calls the community of believers to "carry each other's burdens" (Galatians 6:2) there several realities to the task.

Reality check 1: you will always need to carry a load

Since humans were made as independent creatures, much of what you do in life, you do alone. You feel pain, think thoughts, and store memories in a unique, individual way. You might struggle with cancer, but even when you share your experience with another person with cancer, your own story stands independent of theirs. It's strange to say this, but in one sense it's true: you will live your life on your own.

In Galatians 6:2, Paul directs believers to the high calling of community and to "carry each other's burdens," and yet later in the passage, he adds: "If anyone thinks they are something when they are not, they deceive themselves. Each one should test their own actions. Then they can take pride in themselves alone, without comparing themselves to someone else, *for each one should carry their own load*" (Galatians 6:3–5; emphasis added). Whatever you do to cultivate a sense of community, you still have to act as one person.

Reality check 2: knowing that humans are created to function independently, you are also meant to grow in relationships and work together

The idea is that when we carry each other's burdens, we grow into the image of God's plan. When you come alongside and help a sister or a brother, it is a way to deepen the nature of the community. The task is not to carry someone else's burden but to share the burden or ease their struggle by helping.

If you are carrying something and you trip, the shifting weight will throw you even further off balance. You don't need a physics lessons to tell you that you will need some help to share the burden or help sustain, support, and assist. Sometimes helping stabilize the load allows the burden bearer to negotiate the challenge. When someone staggers, we help steady the load. If someone is straining, we help bear the burden. And if they stumble, we lift them up. Helping fellow believers carry the weight of their troubles is one of the chief practical duties that ought to consume every Christian.

Reality check 3: in a community, when someone shares the load, the collective support is felt around the world

Many will say, "It's a small world" when they describe how connected people are around the globe. When you show up in any part of the world and worship, there is a good chance that you might meet someone who knows a friend or a friend of a friend. When you share the load of another believer, the ripple effect influences lives around the world. As you are connected to others, the sense of collaboration impacts the whole. In Galatians 5:14, Paul reminded his readers: "For the entire law is fulfilled in keeping this one command: 'Love your neighbor as yourself.' "

Clearly, sometimes the burden feels impossible to carry. Everyone hauls baggage around, and the help we offer one another changes everything. As you seek out opportunities to share the burden of a friend, don't forget that you can ask for help with your burden, as well, when it seems like the weight is too heavy.

INSIDE OUT

- How do you define a burden?
- What are the potential benefits of carrying one another's burdens?
- How can we lift the burden of someone we know?
- Consider the following texts:
    - Carry each other's burdens, and in this way you will fulfill the law of Christ. If anyone thinks they are something when they are not, they deceive themselves. Each one should test their own actions. Then they can take pride in themselves alone, without comparing

themselves to someone else, for each one should carry their own load (Galatians 6:2–5).

- Anyone who does not provide for their relatives, and especially for their own household, has denied the faith and is worse than an unbeliever (1 Timothy 5:8).

- The Lord answered him, "You hypocrites! Doesn't each of you on the Sabbath untie your ox or donkey from the stall and lead it out to give it water? Then should not this woman, a daughter of Abraham, whom Satan has kept bound for eighteen long years, be set free on the Sabbath day from what bound her?" (Luke 13:15, 16).

- Then Peter said, "Silver and gold I do not have, but what I do have I give you. In the name of Jesus Christ of Nazareth, walk." Taking him by the right hand, he helped him up, and instantly the man's feet and ankles became strong (Acts 3:6, 7).

33. SPEAK THE TRUTH

Therefore each of you must put off falsehood and speak truthfully to your neighbor, for we are all members of one body. . . . Do not let any unwholesome talk come out of your mouths, but only what is helpful for building others up according to their needs, that it may benefit those who listen.
—Ephesians 4:25, 29

Whether it's foul, vulgar language, senseless profanity, or sacrilegious words—all unwholesome talk is to be avoided. Even though culture tells us that certain words are acceptable, Paul reminds us that certain language is never acceptable for Christ's followers to use. "Unwholesome talk" in the Bible comes from a word describing something that smells rotten. Jesus describes the nature of a tree, saying, "Make a tree good and its fruit will be good, or make a tree bad and its fruit will be bad, for a tree is recognized by its fruit" (Matthew 12:33).

In another passage, Paul counsels readers, "Check your words. Check your heart" (see 2 Corinthians 13:5). He goes so far as to specify what is best for us to think about, "Finally, brothers and sisters, whatever is true, whatever is noble, whatever is right, whatever is pure, whatever is lovely, whatever is admirable—if anything is excellent or praiseworthy—think about such things" (Philippians 4:8). This must make us stop and ask ourselves, "What is the nature of my conversation, words, and what I say out loud?"

Let's do a short exercise along these lines:

The first round

Take an inventory of your conversations with others and your own thoughts. Do you find unwholesome talk in your daily life? If you do, you are not alone. Know that in your heart two voices, two impulses are seeking to influence how you choose to live your life. One—your conscience—is God calling you to follow His ways. It is lovely, good, and true. The other is your selfish and sinful heart; it has a love for disguise and a propensity to hurt others. Now, if you think you are fine because you are mostly "OK," you are deceived. And if you think you are a lost cause, you are equally deceived. The good news is that Christ has made a way to overcome sin, self-righteousness, and abject despair (Romans 8; 2 Corinthians 3:1–6; 2 Corinthians 5:17–21; Ephesians 3:11, 12).

The second round

Remove unwholesome talk and practice self-control in your speech. Here are several exercises:

- *Ask God to help you silence your idle chatter. If we ask, He will give us wisdom for our interactions with others.* You might find that most conversations are about temporary things: weather, sports, fashion, entertainment, and any other trivial subject. Of course, there is nothing essentially wrong about trivial conversations, but the goal is to practice silencing the extra banter in order to distinguish common trivia from the higher themes. Sometimes, you need to silence your idle chatter.
- *Eradicate gossip.* Gossip can be sharing or "updating" someone about the events surrounding others and the ups and downs of the people you know. Again, there is nothing immoral about knowing what is happening in the neighborhood; however, practicing restraint on gossiping strengthens your friendships.
- *Spend time on inner reflection instead of expressing your opinion, commenting, or voicing your stance on issues.* When you have an opportunity to speak, and a clever phrase about a topic comes to mind, reflect quietly instead of speaking. In thinking about the issue, you might consider why the problem is important to you. Sometimes it is easy to roll your eyes or make a cynical or sarcastic comment, but instead, remind yourself quietly why your conviction is so important to humanity. And save your thoughts for another day.

The third round

Cultivate the best words, thoughts, and conversations that are full of grace and truth. One of the most compelling features of Jesus' ministry is that Jesus saw the potential in others even though He knew their worst. Sometimes confidence and a higher expectation for others can frame what you think about them ultimately. For those who are annoying, consider that they are trying to work too hard for approval. The exercise of seeing the best in people is a helpful habit, but praying for people before you to talk them is a wiser practice. Paul models this process with the Philippian church, saying, "I thank my God every time I remember you. In all my prayers for all of you, I always pray with joy because of your partnership in the gospel from the first day until now, being confident of this, that he who began a good work in you will carry it on to completion until the day of Christ Jesus" (Philippians 1:3–6).

Unwholesome talk is a real, constant struggle in the community of believers. As you lean on God's unchanging grace today, may the atmosphere of heaven stir your heart and mind in your interactions with others.

INSIDE OUT

- Why do you think it is such a struggle to avoid unwholesome talk in our communities?
- What are some ways you can follow Paul's advice in Philippians 4:8 today?
- Consider the following texts:

    - Are we beginning to commend ourselves again? Or do we need, like some people, letters of recommendation to you or from you? You yourselves are our letter, written on our hearts, known and read by everyone. You show that you are a letter from Christ, the result of our ministry, written not with ink but with the Spirit of the living God, not on tablets of stone but on tablets of human hearts.

      Such confidence we have through Christ before God. Not that we are competent in ourselves to claim anything for ourselves, but our competence comes from God. He has made us competent as ministers of a new covenant—not of the letter but of the Spirit; for the letter kills, but the Spirit gives life (2 Corinthians 3:1–6).

    - In him and through faith in him we may approach God with freedom and confidence (Ephesians 3:11, 12).

    - "But I tell you that everyone will have to give account on the day of judgment for every empty word they have spoken. For by your words you will be acquitted, and by your words you will be condemned" (Matthew 12:36, 37).

    - "A good man brings good things out of the good stored up in his heart, and an evil man brings evil things out of the evil stored up in his heart. For the mouth speaks what the heart is full of" (Luke 6:45).

    - "For where your treasure is, there your heart will be also" (Matthew 6:21).

34. SAYING GRACE

Do not let any unwholesome talk come out of your mouths, but only what is helpful for building others up according to their needs, that it may benefit those who listen.
—Ephesians 4:29

Unfortunately, it is all too easy to miscommunicate. Consider the following examples. When people say, "It is what it is," it can mean:

- "I accept the state of the situation, even though I have more questions."
- "I'm surrendering to this situation because it seems ambiguous and complicated."
- "Even though I'm uncomfortable with this situation, I'm resigned to it because I feel defeated or tired of trying."

When someone says something emotionally difficult to hear, and the listener responds by saying, "I'm sorry if you feel that way," the emotion the listener is expressing is not sorrow, regret, or remorse but defensiveness. It is a way to appear compassionate and open-minded; but in fact, they are transferring the problem back to the other person.

Finally, when someone says, "No offense, but . . ." it is often another easy way to be offensive. When convicted about something, many people just declare what they feel—and offend someone. It happens all the time. However, some of the most important words Jesus said were offensive to His hearers. Offend someone if you feel you must, and remember to own the results after sharing a piece of your mind. Don't say, "No offense," because that only offends the listener more and won't be any less hurtful.

Practicing restraint with words requires discipline, but saying the right words involves a higher risk. To avoid certain words and phrases might require you to pause for reflection or even be silent. But finding the right word is a commitment to step deeper into the situation. Paul shifts from counseling his readers to avoid "unwholesome talk" to advocating for speaking proactive words. He calls believers to say "only what is helpful for building others up according to their needs, that it may benefit those who listen" (Ephesians 4:29). We must seek to understand God's grace in order to follow Paul's command.

The Gospel of John introduces the story of Jesus with this summary: "Yet to all who did receive him, to those who believed in his name, he gave the right to become children of God" (John 1:12). The gift of grace is bestowed immediately when "receiving and believing" begins. God's love and mercy do not start when people mature their faith but as they grow. When you are speaking grace-filled words to others, consider the declarations of who you are in Christ in the Word of God:

- "And all are justified freely by his grace through the redemption that came by Christ Jesus" (Romans 3:24).
- "In the same way, count yourselves dead to sin but alive to God in Christ Jesus" (Romans 6:11).
- "The gift of God is eternal life in Christ Jesus our Lord" (Romans 6:23).
- "Therefore, there is now no condemnation for those who are in Christ Jesus, because through Christ Jesus the law of the Spirit who gives life has set you free from the law of sin and death" (Romans 8:1, 2).
- "For I am convinced that neither death nor life, neither angels nor demons, neither the present nor the future, nor any powers, neither height nor depth, nor anything else in all creation, will be able to separate us from the love of God that is in Christ Jesus our Lord" (Romans 8:38, 39).
- "For just as each of us has one body with many members, and these members do not all have the same function, so in Christ we, though many, form one body, and each member belongs to all the others" (Romans 12:4, 5).

When you consider what is declared about you in Christ, there is more to say about a believer in the community of faith than anything can be said about anything. There is no limit to the grace-filled things you can say to others. Perhaps speaking grace to others in detail has a way of helping those good words penetrate even deeper into a person's heart. Whether you speak grace with words of affirmation or you share a difficult message with grace, the words are to be personal, true, and specific.

Even though Peter would, on the eve of his own betrayal of Jesus, promise publicly that he would not deny his Lord, he did it anyway. Jesus' words to Peter were personal, true, and very specific to what Peter would experience. Jesus said, "Simon, Simon, Satan has asked to sift all of you as wheat. But I have prayed for you, Simon, that your faith may not fail. And when you have turned back, strengthen your brothers" (Luke 22:31, 32).

Maybe there are people in your life to whom you can practice speaking grace.

INSIDE OUT

- What are some examples of Christ "tearing down" with His words in order to build up? What about Paul, "tearing down" in order to build up?
- What is the difference between profanity, put-downs, gossip, and cursing? How do Christians engage in or with each of these?
- Which is the main motivation of my conversation—what I want to say or what you need to hear?
- Consider the following texts:

  - Let your conversation be always full of grace, seasoned with salt, so that you may know how to answer everyone (Colossians 4:6).

  - May these words of my mouth and this meditation of my heart be pleasing in your sight, LORD, my Rock and my Redeemer (Psalm 19:14).

  - Who is going to harm you if you are eager to do good? But even if you should suffer for what is right, you are blessed. "Do not fear their threats; do not be frightened." But in your hearts revere Christ as Lord. Always be prepared to give an answer to everyone who asks you to give the reason for the hope that you have. But do this with gentleness and respect, keeping a clear conscience, so that those who speak maliciously against your good behavior in Christ may be ashamed of their slander. For it is better, if it is God's will, to suffer for doing good than for doing evil (1 Peter 3:13–17).

35. BE KIND

Be kind and compassionate to one another, forgiving each other, just as in Christ God forgave you.
—Ephesians 4:32

When someone is nice to you, do you ever wonder if they have a hidden agenda? When someone is generous to you, do you wonder if there is a power play at work? When someone is helpful to you, do you consider whether they want you to owe them a favor?

Motives, on this side of heaven, will be tainted. Selfish reasons can partially influence even our best motives. If it is true that "where your treasure is, there your heart will be also" (Matthew 6:21), then making good choices cultivates a kind heart. Good actions allow your motivation to grow in the right direction.

Can you think of a person in your life who is kind? The Bible counsels us to act with kindness; here are a few examples:

- "But love your enemies, do good to them, and lend to them without expecting to get anything back. Then your reward will be great, and you will be children of the Most High, because he is kind to the ungrateful and wicked" (Luke 6:35).
- "Love is patient, love is kind. It does not envy, it does not boast, it is not proud. It does not dishonor others, it is not self-seeking, it is not easily angered, it keeps no record of wrongs. Love does not delight in evil but rejoices with the truth. It always protects, always trusts, always hopes, always perseveres" (1 Corinthians 13:4–7).
- "Therefore, as God's chosen people, holy and dearly loved, clothe yourselves with compassion, kindness, humility, gentleness and patience" (Colossians 3:12).

The "one another church" will be filled with kind people. Ephesians 4:32 adds two other words to amplify and develop the idea of kindness. The Greek word that is translated as "tenderhearted" (NKJV) is the same word we use for *compassion*, which is a gut-wrenching response to people's needs. Every time the word was used in connection with Jesus, someone who had leprosy was healed or a widow burying her son found a joyous surprise at the end of the funeral procession. The other word that is connected to *kindness* is "forgiving"—especially the type of forgiveness that God gives to you.

Being tenderhearted is an intrinsic response—you have it, or you don't. Forgiveness is more the muscle that you must exercise and grow over time. Take, for example, the concept "forgive and forget." Can you really forget the traumatic things you experience in life? Betrayal. Falsehood. Abuse. Contempt or disrespect. Can you forget those things by forgiving them?

It may seem impossible to "forgive and forget," but perhaps a better way to say it is that forgiveness is "remembering with mercy." However, forgiveness is not a pass to be unaccountable. It is true that there are some people whom you should forgive but not trust again.

Forgiveness is a choice to treat others with kindness, even though they have wronged you. A challenge for the "one another church" is to forgive as God has forgiven you:

- How often has God forgiven? An infinite number of times. "He does not treat us as our sins deserve or repay us according to our iniquities. For as high as the heavens are above the earth, so great is his love for those who fear him; as far as the east is from the west, so far has he removed our transgressions from us" (Psalm 103:10–12).
- How has God forgiven you? Through reconciliation. " 'Come now, let us settle the matter,' says the LORD. 'Though your sins are like scarlet, they shall be as white as snow; though they are red as crimson, they shall be like wool' " (Isaiah 1:18).
- How has God forgiven you? Mercifully. "For I will forgive their wickedness and will remember their sins no more" (Hebrews 8:12).

Motivation? It is in process. Know that the kindness of God is mirrored in the lives of those who are believers. And every moment and every turn on the journey with Christ offers opportunities to deepen the character of "Christ in you, the hope of glory" (Colossians 1:27).

INSIDE OUT

Look at an instance where Peter, who had a history of brashness, impulsivity, and anger, speaks on the topic that he struggled with: "Finally, all of you, be like-minded, be sympathetic, love one another, be compassionate and humble" (1 Peter 3:8)

- How should this advice be taken?
- Read this text again, as well as the context in the surrounding verses, and make a conclusion about Peter's motivation.

- Is he a hypocrite who gets angry at others for the things with which he struggles?
- Is he a guilt-filled sinner who tries to make up for his mistakes by preaching them to others?
- Is he a man who is actively orienting himself in alignment with what God has asked?

36. COMFORT

Therefore encourage one another with these words.
—1 Thessalonians 4:18, NKJV

The short phrase commanding believers to "comfort one another with these words" (1 Thessalonians 4:18, NKJV) might seem like an ominous reference to a bleak situation. Why do they need comfort? And what are the words that will be most helpful?

In places like Thessalonica, a Greek port city, the new believers were converts from paganism who struggled to reconcile old and new beliefs. An added dynamic was the persecution that arose on behalf of Caesar, because some were teaching that Jesus, the resurrected King, was returning soon—within months or a few years. Even though Paul and Silas had to leave Thessalonica quickly, the church flourished, in spite of the persecution. Later on, they counseled the church to "comfort one another" with the truth about death, the Resurrection, the second coming of Jesus, and the great reunion of the family of God.

Imagine being part of a community of faith in the first century. Old and young, rich and poor sharing potluck dinners, funerals, and celebrations of baptism—all while risking harassment from local authorities. Consider the hard moments when people wondered, "Where is Jesus?" or, "When is He coming?" The hardships and joys in the church entwined their hearts together, while Paul presented the life-directing description of the glorious hope.

> Brothers and sisters, we do not want you to be uninformed about those who sleep in death, so that you do not grieve like the rest of mankind, who have no hope. For we believe that Jesus died and rose again, and so we believe that God will bring with Jesus those who have fallen asleep in him. According to the Lord's word, we tell you that we who are still alive, who are left until the coming of the Lord, will certainly not precede those who have fallen asleep. For the Lord himself will come down from heaven, with a loud command, with the voice of the archangel and with the trumpet call of God, and the dead in Christ will rise first. After that, we who are still alive and are left will be caught up together with them in the clouds to meet the Lord in the air. And so we will be with the Lord forever (1 Thessalonians 4:13–17).

Two thousand years later, the same letter encourages believers today. The truth is still in our hearts. As death and trials come, our hearts need to be reminded of the truth.

Read and reflect on some of the words offered to those who are grieving. Some phrases are obviously not helpful for those who are suffering, and others are inaccurate or self-serving. Read the phrases that follow, then read the words of Paul again. What insight is there to discover regarding better things to say or not to say?

A few things not to say:

- "It was God's will."
- "At least they aren't suffering now."
- "Everything happens for a reason."
- "You have to be strong."
- "They wouldn't want you to feel sad."
- "I know how you feel."

Clearly, you understand why these very phrases are *not* comforting. But what is helpful? Some say, "Don't say anything," and there is a whole book of wisdom in those three words; but I would also encourage you to think about what is good and comforting to say (see the verses below for some ideas to get you started). The church in Thessalonica was a wonderful example of a community pulling together in their suffering. Reviewing the truth of the story has a place in bringing comfort and hope. Relying on the truth of this story of hope and knowing the value of a loving community is a good start.

INSIDE OUT

- How do Paul's words bring comfort to you?
- In the verses that follow, pick the one that brings the most courage to you and keep it as a reminder throughout the week:

    - Now if we are children, then we are heirs—heirs of God and co-heirs with Christ, if indeed we share in his sufferings in order that we may also share in his glory (Romans 8:17).

    - Praise be to the God and Father of our Lord Jesus Christ, the Father of compassion and the God of all comfort, who comforts us in all our troubles, so that we can comfort those in any trouble with the comfort we ourselves receive from God. For just as we share abundantly in the sufferings of Christ, so also our comfort abounds through Christ (2 Corinthians 1:3–5).

    - "Now I commit you to God and to the word of his grace, which can build you up and give you an inheritance among all those who are sanctified" (Acts 20:32).

37. SEE THE BEST GOOD

Make sure that nobody pays back wrong for wrong, but always strive to do what is good for each other and for everyone else.
—1 Thessalonians 5:15

Do you read the letters in the Bible as individual pieces or as parts of the whole? The words transcend time and place and speak to our circumstances today. They make up more than a handful of tips for the road ahead—Paul invested his heart in a community of love. Take these examples:

- "But Timothy has just now come to us from you and has brought good news about your faith and love" (1 Thessalonians 3:6).
- "May the Lord make your love increase and overflow for each other and for everyone else, just as ours does for you" (1 Thessalonians 3:12).
- "Now about your love for one another we do not need to write to you, for you yourselves have been taught by God to love each other" (1 Thessalonians 4:9).

As you negotiate difficulties, seek to value the parts that make the community enduring.

The end of the letter to the church in Thessalonica captures a concern for the parts and the whole. Again, the gospel spread from Jerusalem to Judaea and Samaria, and then it moved beyond to the ends of the earth.

Jesus walked among people teaching and working miracles—exhibiting authority over storms, demons, and even death. When Jesus ascended and the Holy Spirit descended on the new believers, a new brand of authority emerged in the way the believers were able to live in a community. In thought and practice, unity and selflessness became a culture inside of a broken world. Life in the Jerusalem community was not perfect, but with the Holy Spirit's guidance, the church flourished. Even though persecution raged against the Christians, they continued to support one another, and God blessed them.

Why did the church flourish under persecution? There were revolutions before, but they vanished when Roman soldiers quieted their passion with swords. However, the Christians multiplied when the pressure came. The story of Christ and the Resurrection was sustained by the way the believers cared for one another. The whole story hinged on the fact that the community of faith in Christ stayed together to worship, pray, eat, work, preach, and give themselves to one another.

Paul wrote a letter to remind them about the relationship of the parts to the whole. Three types of people in the church were noted with special concern at the end of the missive: "Warn those who are idle and disruptive, encourage the disheartened, help the weak, be patient with everyone" (1 Thessalonians 5:14).

The first group to address is the idle and disruptive. The word "idle" means "unruly" or "out of line." They need direct instruction as they are growing in the faith of the church. These are the ones who often act first and think later. The "idle" you shall always have with you, so the apostle gave the church the instruction to warn them, which means everything from exerting positive pressure to grace-filled chastisement or turning them in the right direction.

The second group to address is the disheartened. Those who are disheartened have lost courage or strength. They need support and a morale boost. Courage is not the product of one moment of brilliance; it is the constant and enduring attempt to overcome the hurdles before you. The author of Hebrews calls everyone to "not forget" to encourage those who are learning to develop their courage (see Hebrews 10:25). You don't cultivate courage by receiving platitudes, compliments, or unearned ribbons to prop up your self-esteem. Real encouragement is deep truth combined with unflinching confidence that the disheartened can win. The work for the disheartened is a worthy endeavor.

The third group to help is the weak. Those who are physically and emotionally depleted or sick need helpers. Exercising vigor and the ability to stand is not an option for the weak. Ever have a powerful bout of the flu? You might be young, relatively healthy, smart, charming, and even innovative most of the time—but not when you have the flu. The weak need someone to hold them up. Using your resources, strength, and vitality, be the arms and legs and muscles to move them to a place of healing and safety.

Paul wrote about a time when he was weak: "Three times I pleaded with the Lord to take it away from me. But he said to me, 'My grace is sufficient for you, for my power is made perfect in weakness.' Therefore I will boast all the more gladly about my weaknesses, so that Christ's power may rest on me. That is why, for Christ's sake, I delight in weaknesses, in insults, in hardships, in persecutions, in difficulties. For when I am weak, then I am strong" (2 Corinthians 12:8–10).

All the skills that make up an enviable résumé Paul called "rubbish" (Philippians 3:8, NKJV). In times when the world sees brokenness and suffering, God's grace blossoms into a surprising gift.

When you look at a community of faith, with all the parts in the mix, count all people as parts of the whole—even the ones who seem to struggle to contribute. Consider that their weakness, faintheartedness, or even unruliness will lead to the display of the greatness of God to the world. Paul learned later that weakness is an amphitheater for God's work of redemption.

INSIDE OUT

- When have you needed someone to be patient with you?
- Why do you think it is difficult to be patient with those who are struggling?
- How can you support the three groups described in Paul's exhortation to the church?
- When have you seen God's grace more vivid in someone's weakness rather in their strengths?
- Consider the following texts:

    - But he said to me, "My grace is sufficient for you, for my power is made perfect in weakness." Therefore I will boast all the more gladly about my weaknesses, so that Christ's power may rest on me (2 Corinthians 12:9).

    - Therefore, as we have opportunity, let us do good to all people, especially to those who belong to the family of believers (Galatians 6:10).

    - Dear friend, you are faithful in what you are doing for the brothers and sisters, even though they are strangers to you (3 John 1:5).

38. DEFENSE VERSUS OFFENSE

Make sure that nobody pays back wrong for wrong, but always strive to do what is good for each other and for everyone else.
—1 Thessalonians 5:15

For the faith community, there were two courses of action in responding to seasons of persecution—defense and offense.

Defense
Although it is natural to want to protect yourself from harm, evil or persecution comes in many forms. The early church faced the threat of severe physical harm. The apostles, families, and even children were in danger as "Saul began to destroy the church. Going from house to house, he dragged off both men and women and put them in prison" (Acts 8:3). The trauma of fear and violence is a horror that is never forgotten. Even today, many are tortured, imprisoned, beaten, and murdered because of their loyalty to Jesus. How should you defend yourself from evil? If your life today is all that you have, then it makes sense to avoid, deter, and escape persecution in order to keep your life. It is the nature of hateful people to pursue their cause, so eventually, you will not be able to hide from persecution—what then?

If your life is hidden in Christ, then what can someone do to erase your eternal life in Christ? Nothing, absolutely nothing. It may be scary, but faith grows when the heat is hotter, and the truth of God's Word needs to be very secure in your mind.

Defend yourself from persecution and evil not by avoiding conflict but by putting evil in its proper place—below you. What can evil really do to you? Paul reminds us, "In all these things we are more than conquerors through him who loved us" (Romans 8:37).

Either the Word of God is true, or it's not worth your time. Hear the convincing words of one who was attacked and threatened with a violent death:

- "For I am convinced that neither death nor life, neither angels nor demons, neither the present nor the future, nor any powers, neither height nor depth, nor anything else in all creation, will be able to separate us from the love of God that is in Christ Jesus our Lord" (Romans 8:38, 39).

- "For we who are alive are always being given over to death for Jesus' sake, so that his life may also be revealed in our mortal body. So then, death is at work in us, but life is at work in you" (2 Corinthians 4:11, 12).

So what can they do to you? Your life is hidden in Christ! When you believe this, persecution has no power over you. Also, the need for retaliation is counterproductive. The real revolution comes not by weapons or might but as you love others. When believers returned kindness or forgiveness to their attackers, no power could stand against this almost unbelievable grace.

The maxim from the world of sports also applies to everyday life: "The best defense is a good offense." But is also true for believers in God's kingdom. Paul called the church not to retaliate in self-defense but instead to "always strive to do what is good for each other and for everyone else" (1 Thessalonians 5:15).

Offense

Essentially, with the same single-minded conviction toward evil or persecutors, "pursue what is good both for yourselves and for all" (1 Thessalonians 5:15, NKJV). The story of Christ's way penetrates hostile hearts—keep loving one another, not just because it's a thoughtful strategy or because it sounds like an effective marketing technique. We are to love one another in the community because Jesus taught, "By this everyone will know that you are my disciples, if you love one another" (John 13:35). The lesson is not a concept or a clever idea but a defining action for a believer modeled by Christ. While some will follow instructions, others will follow Christ.

Paul further counseled, "Pursue good . . . for *all*" (1 Thessalonians 5:15, NKJV; emphasis added). Recall the words that Jesus told the disciples at His ascension: "You will be my witnesses in Jerusalem, and in all Judea and Samaria, and to the ends of the earth" (Acts 1:8). Why start near home? Does it seem strange to love your people first and then love others? It's not so strange when you think about a community that is so committed to one another that it compels people to want to be a part of that family.

The same idea is offered in Galatians, where Paul counseled, "Let us not become weary in doing good, for at the proper time we will reap a harvest if we do not give up. Therefore, as we have opportunity, let us do good to all people, especially to those who belong to the family of believers" (Galatians 6:9, 10).

When have you witnessed a faith community who genuinely cares and supports one another well? Wouldn't you be compelled to join?

INSIDE OUT

- Look at your sphere of influence. Does it resemble a warm, hospitable hotel or the local DMV?
- What areas of your life may be keeping people from seeing the grace and love you've been given?
- How can you help refurbish your community so that people want to be a part of it?
- Consider the following texts:

  - Love is patient, love is kind. It does not envy, it does not boast (1 Corinthians 13:4).

  - Be kind and compassionate to one another, forgiving each other, just as in Christ God forgave you (Ephesians 4:32).

  - Therefore, as God's chosen people, holy and dearly loved, clothe yourselves with compassion, kindness, humility, gentleness and patience (Colossians 3:12).

39. THINK TANK

And let us consider how we may spur one another on toward love and good deeds.
—Hebrews 10:24

Do you agree or disagree with the old adage, "There is nothing new under the sun"? This observation about life comes from Ecclesiastes 1:9, but the attitude conveys a cynical expectation about anything that masquerades as "new" or smacks of innovation. There is a sense that life is predictable, offering no unique features in the future. Pretty bleak.

Yet around the world about two thousand think tanks are employing people to read, argue, write, and develop ideas into new applications for life. Some of this work is not about technology or cool gadgets but tackling the greatest issues and problems in life:

- Political and social reform
- Ethics
- Humanitarian questions
- Emergent cultural norms
- Transportation
- Health and wellness
- Financial conundrums

Ultimately, large communities around the world value the work of think tanks and try to implement new ideas and strategies for the problems we face. So things labeled "new" or "new and improved" start with a known idea and assert that it has grown into something better. However you define *new* in your mind, is there a need to summon a group to be a "think tank" community of faith? Apparently, new believers were called to show up at a summit on the endeavor of "good deeds" in relation to the gospel.

In Hebrews, the invitation to the table starts with the phrase, "let us consider how." Yes, the nature of the "think tank" for the church would have several criteria. Consider the key ideas I've gathered from the passage:

- Collaborative: "Let us"
- Practical: "How to do"

- Stimulating: "New way to spark a fire and induce or provoke a response"
- Motivating: "Love, the goal, would be the target and the way to measure the action"
- Action-oriented: "Good deeds are the tangible work that is evident"

"And let us consider how we may spur one another on toward love and good deeds" (Hebrews 10:24).

Perhaps the idea of a "think tank" is a little excessive. If the church today is anything like the communities of faith then, there is a need to plan "new ways" to do the old work of loving people in a tangible way.

Why are good deeds the best method for love? Avoid being too technical about the task, but you will see every good deed change the atmosphere with one action. When a bounty of food is brought to a family's bare cupboard, the whole household is changed. The atmosphere of the room becomes warmer. Words are different. Hope springs from the family members' faces instead of disappointment. The new normal is set higher because of one good deed done in love.

Consider a few examples of good deeds that can elevate someone's day:

- The day before company shows up for a giant gathering, the next-door neighbor is there to clean, prepare food, mow, or run an errand.
- Coworkers interrupt a weekly meeting to bring party hats and cake with candles already lit and sing to a member of the team whose birthday is seven months away but in the summer, when everyone typically forgets. (No one expects a celebration seven months from their birthday—it is a perfect time to do the unexpected!)
- As you go through the drive-through to pick up six burritos, four soft tacos, and two tostadas minus cheese, the attendant hands you your fast food and explains, "The driver ahead paid for your meal."

The last example started a revolution in town by bringing surprises—good surprises—to people who didn't anticipate a gift of love from a stranger. Many communities have some form of this initiative. The one I'm familiar with is called Change the Day. Families, classrooms, businesses, and individuals save their change, which is earmarked for good deeds. The collected money is given to groups of students who spend an hour or two going through the town surprising people with acts of kindness. Most of the time, the good deeds are anonymous, demonstrating that love given unconditionally and without regard for recognition is the best love of all. Yes, you can change the atmosphere with good deeds.

One student was asked, "How do you know that your deeds are going to the neediest or poorest?" The student's answer became the stimulating start for the weekly meeting of the outreach think tank: "Everyone is poor and is in need of something. Whether the car in the drive-through is a minivan with the headlight broken on one side or a new BMW, everyone has been touched by something—eventually, good or bad. Cancer attacks the rich or the poor. Relationships can fall apart in any family. I don't know what people are struggling with—I only know that a good surprise today makes the day better."

Think tanks are needed today! Sometimes it takes time to stimulate the saints with opportunities for good deeds, but the promise is true and the reward is always worth the effort.

INSIDE OUT

- Pick one of the following verses that seems the most applicable to your life now. Challenge yourself during the next week to have the meaning of that verse guide your attitude toward service for the week:
    - Whoever sows to please their flesh, from the flesh will reap destruction; whoever sows to please the Spirit, from the Spirit will reap eternal life. Let us not become weary in doing good, for at the proper time we will reap a harvest if we do not give up. Therefore, as we have opportunity, let us do good to all people, especially to those who belong to the family of believers (Galatians 6:8–10).
    - "Truly I tell you, anyone who gives you a cup of water in my name because you belong to the Messiah will certainly not lose their reward" (Mark 9:41).
    - "Be careful not to practice your righteousness in front of others to be seen by them. If you do, you will have no reward from your Father in heaven.

      "So when you give to the needy, do not announce it with trumpets, as the hypocrites do in the synagogues and on the streets, to be honored by others. Truly I tell you, they have received their reward in full. But when you give to the needy, do not let your left hand know what your right hand is doing, so that your giving may be in secret. Then your Father, who sees what is done in secret, will reward you" (Matthew 6:1–4).

40. FESS UP

Is anyone among you in trouble? Let them pray. Is anyone happy? Let them sing songs of praise. Is anyone among you sick? Let them call the elders of the church to pray over them and anoint them with oil in the name of the Lord. And the prayer offered in faith will make the sick person well; the Lord will raise them up. If they have sinned, they will be forgiven. Therefore confess your sins to each other and pray for each other so that you may be healed. *The prayer of a righteous person is powerful and effective.*

—James 5:13–16; emphasis added

James counsels his readers to do the following:

- If anyone is sick, pray.
- If anyone is cheerful, sing praise.
- If anyone is sick, call the elders and anoint them.
- Pray with faith, and the sick person will be made well.

It's not all that simple, though. The preceding statements are fired out like magic bullets from a machine gun out of control. Sometimes the "cause and effect" approach is a slippery slope when you are referring to healing. So the nature of miracles in regard to the sick and dying remains a common question.

The connection between "confessing your sins to one another" and healing is also perplexing. Instead of teasing out all of the theological angles of miracles, consider the personal experience of confession. Whether you held onto the secret or delayed telling the truth, you probably felt awful—sick inside until you spoke up and confessed. "Fessing up" is a common idiom for confessing your sin, but no matter what phrase you use, the effect of admitting your sin is the same: healing.

Maybe you've experienced some of the physical effects of keeping a secret—fatigue, isolation, depression, and sometimes irrational outbursts. And like a toothache, the pain might subside for a while as the body adjusts to the infection, but soon enough, the tooth will flare up with pain again—sometimes worse than before. When you surrender and fess up to whatever you are struggling with, the truth does set you free (John 8:32).

Sometimes confession is admitting your obvious sins—lying, cheating, and hurting people. But also consider the sins in which you hold back from doing the good things you know you should. You can find healing when you confess that your noble heart needs to come out of hiding. Peter speaks his confession of Jesus as "the Messiah, the Son of the living God" (Matthew 16:16) when the other disciples are holding their tongues. Can you imagine the sense of relief after speaking such a truth? Yes, fessing up brings healing.

When you align your heart with the truth, the world becomes right again. Below are a few confessions young adults have shared:

- I confess anger and resentment for not being chosen first.
- I confess feeling safe enough on my own.
- I confess a love for the world and God at the same time—like dating two people at the same time—and it's wrong.
- I confess the overwhelming need to put on a happy face when I'm dying inside.
- I confess that, in my heart of hearts, I want eternal life with God more than anything, but I don't always live that way.
- I confess my addictions—I don't know how I got so lost. I hope God knows how to find me.
- I confess my need to control everything in my life.
- I confess the missed deeds—the opportunities that I lacked the courage to step out and take.
- I confess the jealousy and envy that runs deep within me.
- I confess the ambition to achieve. I think the pressure is killing everything good that I used to love as a child.

What would happen if more believers in the church would "confess [their] sins to each other" (James 5:16)? What would the community of faith look like if fessing up were an acceptable part of relationships?

INSIDE OUT

- Reflect on the confessions listed earlier. Which confession is the most relevant statement for you today?

- Try writing down your own version of these confessions. What would they look like?
- Consider the following texts:

    - If we confess our sins, he is faithful and just and will forgive us our sins and purify us from all unrighteousness (1 John 1:9).

    - Carry each other's burdens, and in this way you will fulfill the law of Christ (Galatians 6:2).

    - But if we walk in the light, as he is in the light, we have fellowship with one another, and the blood of Jesus, his Son, purifies us from all sin (1 John 1:7).

    - Whoever conceals their sins does not prosper, but the one who confesses and renounces them finds mercy (Proverbs 28:13).

41. NO WHINERS

Offer hospitality to one another without grumbling.

—1 Peter 4:9

Do you recall the first time you ate a haystack? Those who grew up eating haystacks might take for granted the approach used when strategically assembling this meal. Which is best—a precise layering method or the mix-it-all-up salad maneuver? Do you have a preference? Here's one description of a first attempt at haystack assembly:

I was starving. Church went long, I think. I had only gone to church three times before, so I didn't have a good reference point for church length, but I remember being ready for food after the service. I was near the front of the line—visitors were invited first. Across from me, I watched as a girl started to work. She took a plate with single-minded confidence. She was a pro. I was eleven, and new to haystacks, so I watched her closely to learn. She put corn chips on the plate and spread them around, then crushed the large chips into small pieces. Shocked, I stopped and stared for a moment. Then it became clear. Chips first, then beans, cheese, lettuce, tomatoes, onions, olives, salsa, guac, and sour cream! After that first time, I never looked back again.

However, hospitality is about more than food; it has to do with providing a welcoming and loving atmosphere to strangers. Those who love God have a long history of this. The parable of the good Samaritan portrays the perfect example of hospitality as a Samaritan becomes the hero by taking care of the Jewish victim on the road.

Let me share one more example. Jesus tells a parable of the final judgment scene, where people are separated into two groups—the sheep and the goats. Of the sheep, Jesus says:

> Then the King will say to those on his right, "Come, you who are blessed by my Father; take your inheritance, the kingdom prepared for you since the creation of the world. For I was hungry and you gave me something to eat, I was thirsty and you gave me something to drink, I was a stranger and you invited me in, I needed clothes and you clothed me, I was sick and you looked after me, I was in prison and you came to visit me."

> Then the righteous will answer him, "Lord, when did we see you hungry and feed you, or thirsty and give you something to drink? When did we see you a stranger and invite you in, or needing clothes and clothe you? When did we see you sick or in prison and go to visit you?"
>
> The King will reply, "Truly I tell you, whatever you did for one of the least of these brothers and sisters of mine, you did for me" (Matthew 25:34–40).

The sheep passed the test by showing kindness to strangers—a test of how they embraced the character of their King in their daily life. Conversely, you can read the story about the goats, but it is not pretty. The sad, short story relates that the goats saw those who were in need and did *not* respond with love. The King informed the goats of their results:

> "Lord, when did we see you hungry or thirsty or a stranger or needing clothes or sick or in prison, and did not help you?"
>
> He will reply, "Truly I tell you, whatever you did not do for one of the least of these, you did not do for me" (Matthew 25:44, 45).

Clearly, the parable demonstrates the basic function of the church after the Resurrection. The Christian movement would have died quickly if it were not for the hospitality the believers practiced daily. The book of Acts repeatedly describes scenes where showing love to a stranger was a nonnegotiable reality.

Remember the key activities for the community of early believers? "Every day they continued to meet together in the temple courts. They broke bread in their homes and ate together with glad and sincere hearts, praising God and enjoying the favor of all the people. And the Lord added to their number daily those who were being saved" (Acts 2:46, 47). The generous hearts of believers are still on call to be on the lookout for strangers to invite into the fellowship of faith.

INSIDE OUT

- Spend some time in prayer concerning the message of the following verses. Ask God to reveal ways that you can improve in the area of hospitality—and for it to be tested:
    - Keep on loving one another as brothers and sisters. Do not forget to show hospitality to strangers, for by so doing some people have shown hospitality to angels without knowing it (Hebrews 13:1, 2).
    - Share with the Lord's people who are in need. Practice hospitality (Romans 12:13).
    - Do everything without grumbling or arguing (Philippians 2:14).

42. LEVI MATTHEW

Then Levi held a great banquet for Jesus at his house, and a large crowd of tax collectors and others were eating with them.

—Luke 5:29

Do you recall test questions that assess your identification abilities? For example, read from left to right and identify the three items that are similar or in the same group:

Shrew	House	Mouse	Rat
Tree	Cantaloupe	Honeydew	Crenshaw
City police	Doughnut	State police	County sheriff

The basic function is to identify similar things in such a way that you could put them in the same group. In Jesus' time, the list for one group on a test might read:

The angel Gabriel	Robbers	Murderers	Tax collectors

Tax collectors were hated because, though they were Israelites, they took their countrymen's money to support the nation that occupied their land. Tax collectors never had a chance to be respected, liked, or understood.

Matthew was a tax collector, whom Jesus called to be one of His disciples. His calling is short, sweet, and surprisingly uneventful, especially for a guy making a massive career change. The text offers only the basic facts: "After this, Jesus went out and saw a tax collector by the name of Levi sitting at his tax booth. 'Follow me,' Jesus said to him, and *Levi got up, left everything and followed him*" (Luke 5:27, 28; emphasis added). Leaving everything is a huge deal—Matthew's is a riches-to-rags story.

Some decisions you make are the result of great consideration. When you decide to take a job on the East Coast instead of the West, you weigh the pros and cons—the weather, proximity to your friends and family, and access to your personal hobbies and activities. However, the choice to leave a senseless existence to embrace a purposeful lifestyle is an obvious decision. Some belabor the choice; others respond immediately when the call comes. Clearly, Matthew wanted a life with Jesus more than anything else, so "he . . . rose up, and followed Him" (Luke 5:28, NKJV).

The next insight is from what occurred at Matthew's house when he hosted an event in honor of his new Master. The book of Luke captures the party in one sentence, saying, "Then Levi held a great banquet for Jesus at his house, and a large crowd of tax collectors and others were eating with them" (Luke 5:29).

The hospitality is described as "a great feast" (NKJV), which called many people together for a celebration. It seems likely that the feast was to intentionally invite "outsiders" into the kingdom of Jesus. The group gathered at Matthew's house was a large company of tax collectors lounging around, seemingly unaware that the gathering was problematic for some.

Some of the religious leaders complained about Jesus' presence at Matthew's celebration. Their complaint was that no spiritual person would socialize with these outcasts. Clearly, the categories were very narrow for Pharisees and scribes. Jesus responded to the complaint with a question and a prompt answer:

> "Why do you eat and drink with tax collectors and sinners?"
>
> Jesus answered them, "It is not the healthy who need a doctor, but the sick. I have not come to call the righteous, but sinners to repentance" (Luke 5:30–32).

The story ends abruptly, but the message of Christ had found a place in the heart of Matthew. Matthew's life transition is cataloged as one of the greatest examples of the transforming work Jesus does in our lives when we choose to follow Him. Consider the themes in Matthew that are unique and not mentioned in Luke and John:

- The genealogy of Jesus includes five unlikely women. Tamar was a Canaanite. Rahab was a prostitute in Jericho. Ruth was Moabite. Bathsheba was originally married to Uriah the Hittite. Mary was an unmarried woman, chosen to bear the Messiah. These women had complex relationships, and true to form, Matthew's Gospel highlights outsiders becoming insiders.
- The call to the disciples in the Great Commission highlights its global purpose: "Therefore go and make disciples of *all nations*" (Matthew 28:19; emphasis added). The message is for all people.
- The parables in Matthew highlight that the kingdom of God is handed off from the Jews to "outsiders."

Here are two more examples:

- "When Jesus heard this, he was amazed and said to those following him, 'Truly I tell you, I have not found anyone in Israel with such great faith. I say to you that many will come from the east and the west, and will take their places at the feast with Abraham, Isaac and Jacob in the kingdom of heaven. But the subjects of the kingdom will be thrown outside, into the darkness, where there will be weeping and gnashing of teeth' " (Matthew 8:10–12).

- "Truly I tell you, the tax collectors and the prostitutes are entering the kingdom of God ahead of you. For John came to you to show you the way of righteousness, and you did not believe him, but the tax collectors and the prostitutes did. And even after you saw this, you did not repent and believe him" (Matthew 21:31, 32).

There is a message for you today, as you are called to RSVP to the invitation to follow Christ as one of His own—will you leave everything and follow Jesus? Why wait? Everyone is invited. The whiners, grumblers, and murmurers either walk out or join the feast. There are many things we can find to complain about today; however, the group who focuses on the sweet gospel message of Christ will endure to the end.

INSIDE OUT

- Why do you think Jesus chose Matthew? Is there anything in the Gospels about Matthew that gives us a clue?
- How would you describe Matthew to your friends?
- When have you witnessed someone being called to leave everything to follow Christ?
- Consider the following texts:

    - "In the same way, those of you who do not give up everything you have cannot be my disciples" (Luke 14:33).

    - Do not love the world or anything in the world. If anyone loves the world, love for the Father is not in them. For everything in the world—the lust of the flesh, the lust of the eyes, and the pride of life—comes not from the Father but from the world. The world and its desires pass away, but whoever does the will of God lives forever (1 John 2:15–17).

    - Jesus looked at him and loved him. "One thing you lack," he said. "Go, sell everything you have and give to the poor, and you will have treasure in heaven. Then come, follow me" (Mark 10:21).

    - "For whoever wants to save their life will lose it, but whoever loses their life for me and for the gospel will save it" (Mark 8:35).

43. MARTHA VERSUS MARY

As Jesus and his disciples were on their way, he came to a village where a woman named Martha opened her home to him.
—Luke 10:38

What is the most meaningful kitchen in your memories? Perhaps your current home's kitchen is, by far, your favorite place. Maybe your grandma's loving preparation of food or a friend's table set for tea holds that special place in your heart. How would you describe the style of your favorite kitchen?

The country farmhouse kitchen is inviting, featuring an open concept and bringing space, warmth, and function together in one room. It seems to say, "There is beauty in good food and togetherness. Perfection is not the goal."

Perhaps you prefer the modern kitchen, which features a sophisticated, sleek, and clean look that declares, "Life doesn't have to be messy." This kitchen will have plenty of cupboards and hidden areas to store all the clutter.

Or maybe the cottage kitchen has all the charm and love you will ever need. Space is not the most important value; trendy colors and materials are secondary to interesting and unique qualities. This kitchen recalls, "There is a story about that spoon."

A sense of community is connected to food, family and friends, and memorable places. Bethany is a special place in the story of Christ. There are at least three events written in the Bible that take place at Martha's home, but one in particular shares a timeless lesson from the table.

Review the story and consider a few lessons:

> As Jesus and his disciples were on their way, he came to a village where a woman named Martha opened her home to him. She had a sister called Mary, who sat at the Lord's feet listening to what he said. But Martha was distracted by all the preparations that had to be made. She came to him and asked, "Lord, don't you care that my sister has left me to do the work by myself? Tell her to help me!"

"Martha, Martha," the Lord answered, "you are worried and upset about many things, but few things are needed—or indeed only one. Mary has chosen what is better, and it will not be taken away from her" (Luke 10:38–42).

Without a doubt, Martha cares about hospitality, doing well, and working hard. Yet Martha is under the microscope while Mary gets a pass. Consider a few lessons we can learn at Martha's table:

- *Hospitality is the central feature in the home.* The sense of security, warmth, and love shines through Martha's efforts. There is more to the essence of "home" than food.
- *Comparing yourself to others is unwise.* Martha is happy cooking, yet feels unhappy when she compares her work with Mary's ease. This comparison takes her down a slippery slope.
- *Single-mindedness is not a weakness but a strength.* Martha had many cares, and they all were equal—cleaning the carrots, Jesus, what was baking in the oven, the weather, sweeping the floor, and remembering the butter. If all things are equally important, then nothing is *really* important.

Part of maturing is learning to lose and win well. You can't have equal safety *and* sport in the same car; casual *and* classic dress; or a lifestyle of ambition *and* leisure. The idea is to know the order of things and be satisfied with the first things being first. Mary had learned this lesson and focused on building her relationship with Jesus. Martha's heart needed a slight remodel. It's not a personality weakness or strength. Martha wasn't a monster; she simply cared about many things. Learning to let go of lesser things in order to win the one thing you need the most can be difficult, yet it is undoubtedly the most important lesson to learn.

INSIDE OUT

- Of Martha and Mary, whom do you relate to the most?
- What was it about Mary that impressed Jesus?
- Where is the balance between Mary and Martha's actions that we should strive for?
- Consider the following texts:

    - Finally, brothers and sisters, whatever is true, whatever is noble, whatever is right, whatever is pure, whatever is lovely, whatever is admirable—if anything is excellent or praiseworthy—think about such things (Philippians 4:8).

    - Above all, love each other deeply, because love covers over a multitude of sins. Offer hospitality to one another without grumbling (1 Peter 4:8, 9).

- “Enter through the narrow gate. For wide is the gate and broad is the road that leads to destruction, and many enter through it. But small is the gate and narrow the road that leads to life, and only a few find it” (Matthew 7:13, 14).

44. AIM HIGHER

Late in the afternoon the Twelve came to him and said, "Send the crowd away so they can go to the surrounding villages and countryside and find food and lodging, because we are in a remote place here." He replied, "You give them something to eat." They answered, "We have only five loaves of bread and two fish—unless we go and buy food for all this crowd." (About five thousand men were there.) But he said to his disciples, "Have them sit down in groups of about fifty each."

—Luke 9:12–14

There is only one miracle that all four Gospels mention—the feeding of the five thousand.

Although the people were not gathered around a physical table in the scene, the story provides us with an example of true community. In this community, the disciples learned to aim higher.

Before you read and considered the story of the feeding of the five thousand, how would you have defined a miracle? A surprising event explained only by the work of a supernatural being or divine agency? An act of God? An extraordinary occurrence attributed to the action of ultimate power?

Although miracles today may appear different, the principle is timeless: what is impossible for people is possible for God.

On the day when five thousand men—plus women and children—were fed, the miraculous occurred, in a couple of ways. Jesus prayed and multiplied the food for many, and the only person who had plenty gave it away for others.

When you are selfish and protect your resources, you will lose more than you think

When the disciples surveyed the scene, their assessment and solution are surprising. The disciples suggested, "Send the crowd away so they can go to the surrounding villages and countryside and find food and lodging, because we are in a remote place here" (Luke 9:12). After witnessing the lame walking, the blind seeing, the lepers cleansed, and the dead raised, why would the disciples tell Jesus to send people away?

Furthermore, after searching for food among the people, they found only one person who had five loaves of bread and two fish? Something was very, very fishy! After making the call and gathering the inventory, the Bible stated, "About five thousand men were there" (Luke 9:14).

You can look at the situation from the standpoint of, "That's a lot of people to feed." Or, "That's a lot of people; surely someone brought food." Is it possible that the people were holding on to their own food? Only a young boy offered to share his food.

Either way, the crowds were organized into groups of fifties, Jesus prayed and blessed the food—and the disciples handed out food, which had multiplied exponentially. In the end, there were twelve baskets left over. Why twelve? Maybe at least part of the lesson was for the disciples to aim higher.

If you look to yourself for resources, you will be wanting. If your only solutions are human answers, you will turn up short. Jesus, on another occasion, promised, "With man this is impossible, but not with God; all things are possible with God" (Mark 10:27). This was not just a pep talk at halftime. Truly, "all things are possible with God."

When the angel Gabriel informed Mary that she was going to have a baby—the Messiah—Mary had questions. Gabriel replied, "Even Elizabeth your relative is going to have a child in her old age, and she who was said to be unable to conceive is in her sixth month. For no word from God will ever fail" (Luke 1:36, 37). In other words, the miraculous is the way things go in heaven—get used to it!

Selflessness means always looking higher for other options
The boy who offered the food was a remarkable child. Consider the odds of having only one child out of more than five thousand people who brought food. It is humbling to witness a child exhibit the selfless willingness to gladly offer up everything at his disposal for others.

When Jesus had the bread and the fish, "[He looked] up to heaven, he gave thanks and broke them" (Luke 9:16). Aim higher.

The disciples looked to their own hands—and found nothing. Packing up twelve baskets of leftovers, the disciples might have said to each other, "We need to aim higher."

The child had come to that conclusion first. "Always aim higher."

INSIDE OUT

- Has there been a time when your expectations have been exceeded?
- Were you prepared for that surprise in some way?
- Do you think the following phrase is true: "If your goals don't require the work of God, you're not aiming high enough"? Why or why not?
- Consider the following texts:

  - Peter looked straight at him, as did John. Then Peter said, "Look at us!" So the man gave them his attention, expecting to get something from them.

    Then Peter said, "Silver or gold I do not have, but what I do have I give you. In the name of Jesus Christ of Nazareth, walk." Taking him by the right hand, he helped him up, and instantly the man's feet and ankles became strong (Acts 3:4–7).

  - "Fellow Israelites, listen to this: Jesus of Nazareth was a man accredited by God to you by miracles, wonders and signs, which God did among you through him, as you yourselves know" (Acts 2:22).

45. SEPARATE ONES

But whatever were gains to me I now consider loss for the sake of Christ. What is more I consider everything a loss because of the surpassing worth of knowing Christ Jesus my Lord, for whose sake I have lost all things. I consider them garbage, that I may gain Christ.
—Philippians 3:7, 8

Imagine your assignment was to write the story of Jesus and the early church, much like the story we find in Luke and Acts. What would you focus on? What angle or themes would you emphasize to make the message approachable for readers? Perhaps you might add examples of art, poems, and songs or stories and just set your creation out randomly on the coffee table. Doctor Luke doesn't do random. If you were his patient, you would be thankful that your physician was more strategic and careful about your body. But if *you* were to write the story of Jesus and the events of the early church, what would you share?

- What human subjects would you research and examine?
- What great events would capture the essence of Jesus and His believers?
- What would be the ultimate conclusion you would hope to accomplish by sharing this gospel?

Do you envision writing the encounters of Jesus and the Pharisees? Luke has three sections where the Pharisees harass Jesus. *Pharisee* is a synonym for *legalist* in some circles, but in the Bible, it is a term for a pious person or, more technically, "The separate ones." Because of their uncompromising devotion to the law, they sought to align themselves as perfectly as possible with God's will. God's will appeared to be narrower as the volume of their laws for "being in it" increased.

Be patient with the Pharisee types you encounter. The most problematic Pharisee is the one who keenly and quickly recognizes the legalist in others but is blind to their own tendencies. Jews revered the Pharisees for their devotion but found their piety unapproachable. Their power and influence within the Jewish community were unmatched, and Jesus came to set the record straight regarding what was God's will and what is pleasing in God's sight.

Between the four Gospels, there are three stories about Pharisees inviting Jesus to the table. Don't be a Pharisee and try to assume you know all of their motivations, but take the stories as they are—insights to a group of people who believed compromise equaled unacceptable failure, who were remarkably passionate and attentive to the details. At the end of the day, a Pharisee invited Jesus over for a meal. Some of the table talk turned into a lesson about table manners as probably happens at your house occasionally. "When one of the Pharisees invited Jesus to have dinner with him, he went to the Pharisee's house and reclined at the table" (Luke 7:36).

The first table story is about reconciliation: "When Jesus had finished speaking, a Pharisee invited him to eat with him; so he went in and reclined at the table" (Luke 11:37). While Jesus and the Pharisee were at the table, a woman came and anointed Him with oil. The critics considered the woman to be one with a dubious reputation, but Jesus responded with a beautiful devotional on forgiveness and mercy. At the end of the story, Jesus said to the woman, "Your faith has saved you; go in peace" (Luke 7:50).

The second table story is about the inner life and the heart. The Pharisees complained about the disciples' lax mealtime ritual—according to them, the disciples didn't wash properly. Because Jesus didn't wash His hands the same way as they did, they were offended. Jesus' response was simple and clear. He declared, "Now then, you Pharisees clean the outside of the cup and dish, but inside you are full of greed and wickedness" (Luke 11:39).

The third table story is about the invitation for all to be welcome at the table. The story is strange. The atmosphere is charged—anything could happen. The Pharisees needed Jesus to confirm before "witnesses" the charges that were percolating in their minds already. The Bible announces, "There in front of him was a man suffering from abnormal swelling of his body" (Luke 14:2). Surely, a Pharisee, who would be very careful about cleanliness, would be aware of the sick man in the room. Jesus spoke directly to the issue: "Is it lawful to heal on the Sabbath or not?" (Luke 14:3). Sometimes questions are tricky, and silence is the safe answer. Jesus chastised them because of the fact that they cared for their animals but dismissed a person in need.

After several parables, the message is clear: invite everyone, because ultimately the kingdom of God will naturally compel all people to join the table. The end of the parable is still open for a response and a conclusion. The tables were turned again later when, after the Resurrection, a few Pharisees showed up on the other side of the fight.

Nicodemus, who sought a conference with Jesus at night, learned about being born again. Later, Nicodemus tried to intercede for Jesus when the Pharisees were plotting His death and then again after the Crucifixion. Nicodemus risked his life by paying for the spices used for the burial of Jesus.

Gamaliel, who was a master teacher and a revered leader, advised the angry mob of Jewish leaders to leave the disciples of Jesus alone. He concluded: "Therefore, in the present case I advise you: Leave these men alone! Let them go! For if their purpose or activity is of human origin, it will fail. But if it is from God, you will not be able to stop these men; you will only find yourselves fighting against God" (Acts 5:38, 39).

By far, the most famous Pharisee in the Bible is Saul of Tarsus, who learned that God's grace is stronger than anything. The community of faith will grow in God's timing—in the meantime, have patience with one another.

INSIDE OUT

- Have you observed the Pharisee attitude in the church today?
- Have you witnessed this attitude in yourself, especially in interactions with people who differ from you in practice or belief?
- How does the message of the table affect how you interact with those people?
- Consider the following texts:

    - The true light that gives light to everyone was coming into the world. He was in the world, and though the world was made through him, the world did not recognize him. He came to that which was his own, but his own did not receive him. Yet to all who did receive him, to those who believed in his name, he gave the right to become children of God—children born not of natural descent, nor of human decision or a husband's will, but born of God (John 1:9–13).

    - "And the Father who sent me has himself testified concerning me. You have never heard his voice nor seen his form, nor does his word dwell in you, for you do not believe the one he sent. You study the Scriptures diligently because you think that in them you have eternal life. These are the very Scriptures that testify about me, yet you refuse to come to me to have life.

      "I do not accept glory from human beings, but I know you. I know that you do not have the love of God in your hearts" (John 5:37–42).

46. MY TABLE

When Jesus reached the spot,
he looked up and said to him, "Zacchaeus,
come down immediately. I must stay
at your house today." So he came down
at once and welcomed him gladly.
All the people saw this and began to mutter,
"He has gone to be the guest of a sinner."
—Luke 19:5–7

"Arrested for murder . . ."

"Tried and convicted with a life-sentence term . . ."

"After ten years in prison, the convicted criminal is released . . ."

If you read this sequence of stories in the newspaper, would you be angry? What if the freed prisoner had been exonerated after being wrongly imprisoned for a crime he didn't commit?

The Innocence Project is an organization that works to exonerate those who are innocent but wrongly convicted by such things as false confession and eyewitness misidentification. They use new technology and DNA to test evidence, which previously was not possible.

What is worse: releasing a person who is guilty or convicting an innocent person? The first rule of law is to protect the person from being judged guilty when they are innocent. If criminals squeeze through the cracks of justice, their reward is still coming. As it is written in Galatians, "Do not be deceived: God cannot be mocked. A man reaps what he sows. Whoever sows to please their flesh, from the flesh will reap destruction; whoever sows to please the Spirit, from the Spirit will reap eternal life" (Galatians 6:7, 8).

The stories of people who are misunderstood, misidentified, misjudged, and ultimately mistreated are heartwrenching. In life, being known is hard work. First impressions are not at all fair or correct. Sadly, many catch a glimpse of the person but not of the whole, which causes pain because we are created to know and be known.

When have you felt like you were misunderstood? Remember the story of Zacchaeus? At the end of his story, Jesus invited Himself to a meal at Zacchaeus's house. We have very few details about the conversation that took place during that meal, but one declaration stands out clearly. Zacchaeus stated, "Look, Lord! Here and now I give half of my possessions to the poor, and if I have cheated anybody out of anything, I will pay back four times the amount" (Luke 19:8).

Although society had judged him due to his choice to become a tax collector—and ultimately because he cheated people by charging more than was necessary—Zacchaeus presented his case to a higher court, to the One who would see him in complete truth. His words were not laced with anger or self-righteousness but with repentance and humility. Jesus understood Zacchaeus. Truly, the words of Jesus to Zacchaeus are more valuable than riches: "Today salvation has come to this house, because this man, too, is a son of Abraham" (Luke 19:9).

Prejudice is born when people prejudge others. The world needs a generation who will do more than simply not judge others—it needs a generation who will take the time to get to know others or a situations and seek understanding. I am reminded of the following examples:

- Mary of Bethany, for her teachable spirit
- Nathanael, for his thoughtful transparency
- The unknown widow, who arrested the attention of Jesus by quietly giving everything she had
- The Roman soldier and the Canaanite mother, who were both, in faith, seeking healing for someone else
- Peter, who opened his mouth when others were silent and spoke words that started a church
- John the Baptist, who was a voice for repentance and reformation in preparation for the coming Messiah
- A Samaritan leper, who moved the heart of God by returning to say thank you for Jesus' healing.

All were misunderstood, initially. All were declared children of God. Perhaps there is a lesson for all who trust their first impressions or follow the crowds' perceptions. It might be that there are many more who are candidates for the community of faith than we suppose at first glance.

INSIDE OUT

- Do you know people who are easily misunderstood?

- Do intentions or results matter? Both?
- Here are some verses in which Jesus directly compliments people who were misunderstood:

  - "I tell you, among those born of women there is no one greater than John; yet the one who is least in the kingdom of God is greater than he" (Luke 7:28).

  - "Martha, Martha," the Lord answered, "you are worried and upset about many things, but few things are needed—or indeed only one. Mary has chosen what is better, and it will not be taken away from her" (Luke 10:41, 42).

47. PASSOVER MEAL

When the hour came, Jesus and his apostles reclined at the table. And he said to them, "I have eagerly desired to eat this Passover with you before I suffer. For I tell you, I will not eat it again until it finds fulfillment in the kingdom of God."

—Luke 22:14–16

The sound of a car crash.

The smell of freshly baked bread.

The sight of the ocean.

Anything—sights, sounds, smells—can trigger your memory of events if they are somehow linked to the experience. During the Passover Feast, the Lord shared a meal with His disciples that recalled the night of Israel's escape from bondage. With Communion, Jesus urged His disciples to remember the sacrifice He would soon make, saying, "This is my body given for you; do this in remembrance of me" (Luke 22:19). The Bible also says that "in the same way, after the supper he took the cup, saying, 'This cup is the new covenant in my blood, which is poured out for you' " (Luke 22:20). In fact, we continue to celebrate the experience of salvation through the Lord's Supper. Memory is critical to every aspect of life, but especially the spiritual life.

Regardless of what we may or may not know about human memory, it is true that believers are called to be intentional about what we remember. Why? Because if we don't remember, we will forget. Think of all the stories in the Bible where people learned, experienced, or discovered something so real, but over time they failed to remember. The Savior connected two simple attributes of everyday life—bread and wine—to the gift of eternal life made available by the Cross. It connects everyday life to eternal life. The Lord's Supper is about linking our memory to that which is most meaningful. This is not just to avoid forgetting but to relive it as though it just happened. This makes it real.

Every detail of the Passover meal prompted the people to remember the meaning of the Exodus:

- The lamb had to be killed, and the blood poured out, because "the life of a creature is in the blood" (Leviticus 17:11).
- The unleavened bread made quickly and eaten quickly mirrored the Israelites' hasty escape from Egypt. There was no time to allow the leavened dough to rise, so they made unleavened bread.
- A bowl of salt water represented the tears they shed while captive in Egypt and the waters of the Red Sea through which they miraculously escaped.
- Bitter herbs were to awaken in them a sense of the bitterness of slavery.
- Also, there was a paste of apples, nuts, and pomegranates with sticks of cinnamon; this portrayed the bricks of clay and straw they made as slaves.
- The wine, or the juice of the grape, represents the joy in celebration of being free. Everyone would drink a full four cups of juice.

Every detail was carefully prepared and ordered for a reason—not only to remind the participants of the event but also to help them experience it. Every child of Israel was to celebrate every detail—to experience the oppression, bitterness, injustice, and the joy of being set free—as though it had just happened to *them*. Every generation would relive this experience every year, so they would never forget the despair of captivity and the joy of salvation.

When Jesus bent down and washed His disciples' feet, the lesson in humility was unmistakable. To make sure they had learned, Jesus asked, "Do you understand what I have done for you?" (John 13:12). The Lord wanted to fasten in the memory of the disciples the quality they would need most—a servant's heart. Even after the Resurrection, Jesus appeared to two travelers on the road, and they did not recognize Him until late in the day when they invited Him in to eat. "When he was at the table with them, he took bread, gave thanks, broke it and began to give it to them. Then their eyes were opened and they recognized him, and he disappeared from their sight" (Luke 24:30, 31). In this one image of bread, hands, and words of thanks, the grace and power of Christ's identity is realized.

It's safe to say that when Jesus invites His followers to remember something, the memory must be important. As you celebrate the Lord's Supper, fix your mind on what God wants you to remember. Taste it. Testify to it. Sing about it. Feel the peace and share the joy of God's grace, and remember never to forget what Christ has done.

INSIDE OUT

- What are the things you tend to forget the most? Keys?

Appointments? Directions? Names? What are some practices you do to try to remember successfully?
- Think of three or four of the most unforgettable experiences you have had in your life. How often do those memories emerge? Does the thought of the event come to you automatically, or does something that happens in the course of the day trigger the memory?
- What are the key elements of the celebration of the Lord's Supper?
- How can you make the Lord's Supper meaningful for yourself today?
- Consider the following texts:

  - Is not the cup of thanksgiving for which we give thanks a participation in the blood of Christ? And is not the bread that we break a participation in the body of Christ? Because there is one loaf, we, who are many, are one body, for we all share the one loaf (1 Corinthians 10:16, 17).

  - They devoted themselves to the apostles' teaching and to fellowship, to the breaking of bread and to prayer (Acts 2:42).

  - When he was at the table with them, he took bread, gave thanks, broke it and began to give it to them. Then their eyes were opened and they recognized him, and he disappeared from their sight (Luke 24:30, 31).

48. EMMAUS MEAL

When he was at the table with them, he took bread, gave thanks, broke it and began to give it to them. Then their eyes were opened and they recognized him, and he disappeared from their sight.
—Luke 24:30, 31

It seems like every pivotal moment in life involves a seven-mile walk. Take the disciples on the road to Emmaus. Are you ready? Let's read about their trip:

> As they talked and discussed these things with each other, Jesus himself came up and walked along with them; but they were kept from recognizing him.
>
> He asked them, "What are you discussing together as you walk along?"
>
> They stood still, their faces downcast (Luke 24:15–18).

Throughout your journey with God, you will experience the seventh mile. Seven miles is not easy but possible. Will you move forward even when you don't know why you're traveling? Will you stay close and listen even when it doesn't make sense? Will you come to the table and wait? The work of the community is to stay together and to keep moving forward.

Every good relationship has a seven-mile walk. Every career shift into a new calling has a seven-mile walk ahead. Every semester at a university has a seven-mile walk for a student. The freedom from a destructive habit or an addiction has a seven-mile walk to the victory. Every decision to experience reconciliation has a seven-mile walk to peace. And even the spiritual renewal that you longed for still awaits you—it's about seven miles ahead.

There is a *trudging* toward home where your steps are labored. The pace of the two disciples on the road home is painstakingly slow. You have walked this way before, you know how far you have yet to go, and the only way to manage your exhaustion is to pray, focus, and summon every fiber of your strength to take one more step. But, step-by-step, you continue going because the only other option is to give up. The view will never change unless you move forward.

There is a *trying,* when you struggle to make sense of your questions—when you check the facts, define the terms, squeeze your eyes shut to consider other perspectives, and nothing seems to bring clarity. What were the things the disciples were trying to understand? Read the description:

> "What things?" he asked.
>
> "About Jesus of Nazareth," they replied. "He was a prophet, powerful in word and deed before God and all the people. The chief priests and our rulers handed him over to be sentenced to death, and they crucified him; but we had hoped that he was the one who was going to redeem Israel. And what is more, it is the third day since all this took place. In addition, some of our women amazed us. They went to the tomb early this morning but didn't find his body. They came and told us that they had seen a vision of angels, who said he was alive. Then some of our companions went to the tomb and found it just as the women had said, but they did not see Jesus" (Luke 24:19–24).

Does it sound as though they were defeated? "We had believed . . . We had hoped . . . We had thought . . ." All of the information is not enough. Today, you might have all the answers, but they still don't fit because the solution is not information but a Person. Sometimes you need to keep walking.

There is a *turning* of the pages, when you are not seeking information but a revelation. You can sense that your struggle is active, but you don't know how or why. The process of revelation is not magic but a willingness to stay until God speaks on His own terms and in His own timing. Notice the Bible study is not about events and truths but Jesus as the Message and the Messenger. " 'Did not the Messiah have to suffer these things and then enter his glory?' And beginning with Moses and all the Prophets, he explained to them what was said in all the Scriptures concerning himself" (Luke 24:26, 27).

There is a *timing* in which God reveals Himself. Everything is there for God to unveil the truth to you, but to receive the blessing, you need to be at the table. Instead of sitting in the dark, you must keep walking. When you want to quit because it doesn't make sense, move forward with Jesus instead. When you can't see the way, stay. When they arrived at the house, the disciples were still lost. When you don't know what else to do, gather at the table. "When he was at the table with them, he took bread, gave thanks, broke it and began to give it to them. Then their eyes were opened and they recognized him, and he disappeared from their sight. They asked each other, 'Were not our hearts burning within us while he talked with us on the road and opened the Scriptures to us?' " (Luke 24:30–32).

Sometimes you can attend an event without actually participating in the experience. Sometimes what is true, good, right, and beautiful emerges only if you stay. The revelation will come. The lock clicks, the lights come on, the cloud lifts, and you say, "Now I see. It was right there with me walking down the road."

There is a *telling* of the story. The seven-mile slog is nearing its end, and you feel your second wind urging you to run. "They got up and returned at once to Jerusalem. There they found the Eleven and those with them, assembled together and saying, 'It is true! The Lord has risen and has appeared to Simon.' Then the two told what had happened on the way, and how Jesus was recognized by them when he broke the bread" (Luke 24:33–35).

As you walk on the seven-mile journey home, don't forget to tell the story to others. The sense of community in uncertain times is meant to be shared with others. Telling your story might be the starting point to launch another disciple or two down the road to the best journey ever. See you at the table.

INSIDE OUT

- Why did Jesus appear to those disciples on the road and make such an effort to bring understanding to them?
- Reflect on a time that you felt lost or when things didn't make sense.
- How do you respond when you are in that position?
- Consider the following texts:

  - Trust in the LORD with all your heart,
    and lean not on your own understanding;
in all your ways submit to him,
    and he will make your paths straight (Proverbs 3:5, 6).

  - "It is written in the Prophets: 'They will all be taught by God.' Everyone who has heard the Father and learned from him comes to me" (John 6:45).

  - "All your children will be taught by the LORD, and great will be their peace" (Isaiah 54:13).

49. METAPHORICALLY SPEAKING

Consequently, you are no longer foreigners and strangers, but fellow citizens *with God's people and also members of* his household, *built on the foundation of the apostles and prophets, with Christ Jesus himself as the chief cornerstone. In him the whole building is joined together and rises to become* a holy temple *in the Lord. And in him you too are being built together to become a dwelling in which God lives by his Spirit.*
—Ephesians 2:19–22; emphasis added

In a world where communication comes through various methods, sometimes creating a list is appropriate. But in the ancient world, it was common to use imagery and story to communicate with others. Only the most important message used metaphors and images. A metaphor is a comparison between two things, usually using imagery and descriptive language. Metaphors connect and relate more complex things with familiar ideas. For example:

- "The teaching of the wise is a fountain of life" (Proverbs 13:14).
- "Yet you, LORD, are our Father. We are the clay, you are the potter; we are all the work of your hand" (Isaiah 64:8).
- "The LORD is my shepherd, I lack nothing" (Psalm 23:1). David, knowing about the business of shepherding, turns it around and says, "I am a sheep, and I have a Shepherd."
- "Then Jesus declared, 'I am the bread of life. Whoever comes to me will never go hungry, and whoever believes in me will never be thirsty' " (John 6:35).
- The narrator of the book of Revelation concludes the matter of who God is, saying, "It is done. I am the Alpha and the Omega, the Beginning and the End" (Revelation 21:6).

- "The wind blows wherever it pleases. You hear its sound, but you cannot tell where it comes from or where it is going. So it is with everyone born of the Spirit" (John 3:8).

The apostle Paul offers three images of what it means to be a part of the community of faith.

The first comparison is: "You are no longer foreigners and strangers, but *fellow citizens* with God's people" (Ephesians 2:19; emphasis added). When you travel internationally, you experience being a stranger. There are special lines through customs for strangers. Your passport declares that you identify with another community. The language, the food, the side of the street you walk or drive on—the whole atmosphere may feel foreign. Paul reminds you that your identity is not merely from your country of origin but is from your citizenship in God's nation, and your King is Christ. The key is to remember you are on your way home.

The second metaphor is about being "members of the *household of God*" (Ephesians 2:19, NKJV; emphasis added). The household is your family—your people. The church is God's family, and all the nuances of being a part of your family are like the church. Your family shapes how you see the church, but it doesn't mean that your experience needs to define how you function as a member of the household of faith. Family is a great idea, but the reality is far from perfect—not because people are horrible but because the world is hard, and the effort to love, support, and respect one another is part of a work in process. Your personal relationships with your friends, your spouse, your children, and your parents are growing. The importance of the family can't be underrated today. Recall what Paul charged believers: "Therefore, as we have opportunity, let us do good to all people, especially to those who belong to the family of believers" (Galatians 6:10).

Third, the believers in Christ are like a *temple*. Throughout the history of God's people, Israel, the temple was the center of life. Whether a tent in the desert or Solomon's glorious temple, the sanctuary was the epicenter of life for believers. The whole story of redemption is told through every component of the temple experience. God commanded, "Then have them make a sanctuary for me, and I will dwell among them" (Exodus 25:8). The purpose of the temple is to connect God and people. Period. Then Jesus "became flesh and made his dwelling among us. We have seen his glory, the glory of the one and only Son, who came from the Father, full of grace and truth" (John 1:14). As when Christ ascended and the Holy Spirit fell on the believers, the same grace works now in and through you—for you are a temple today. As it is written, "Don't you know that you yourselves are God's temple and that God's Spirit dwells in your midst?" (1 Corinthians 3:16). If this is true, everything that happens today gives you an opportunity for worshiping, serving, and extending grace to others.
To summarize, the following metaphors paint a picture of what the Christian community should look like:

- The church is like a foreigner making their way home.
- The church is a household of faith, coming together in love.
- The church is people who "are being built together for a dwelling place of God in the Spirit" (Ephesians 2:22, NKJV).

If this is not your experience, then the question is not why but how? How can you travel, live, and function as a conduit of grace? May the Holy Spirit, who is promised to do great things, be unmistakable in your day—today.

INSIDE OUT

- If you were to describe the work of a community of faith with a metaphor, what image would you choose? Here are a few examples to get you started—plant, vehicle, weather, food, recreation, sport.
- Share your metaphor with someone else.
- Consider the following texts:

    - "And I tell you that you are Peter, and on this rock I will build my church, and the gates of Hades will not overcome it" (Matthew 16:18).

    - So in Christ we, though many, form one body, and each member belongs to all the others (Romans 12:5).

    - Then I heard a loud voice in heaven say:
      "Now have come the salvation and the power
         and the kingdom of our God,
         and the authority of his Messiah.
      For the accuser of our brothers and sisters,
         who accuses them before our God day and night,
         has been hurled down.
      They triumphed over him
         by the blood of the Lamb
         and by the word of their testimony;
      they did not love their lives so much
         as to shrink from death" (Revelation 12:10, 11).

50. ALMOST NO-NAMERS

Everyone has heard about your obedience,
so I rejoice because of you; but I want
you to be wise about what is good,
and innocent about what is evil.
The God of peace will soon
crush Satan under your feet.
The grace of our Lord Jesus be with you.
—Romans 16:19, 20

The book of Romans is intimidating. Paul wrote a letter to this church and the content is deep. During one exercise, sixteen young adults were each assigned one of the sixteen chapters of Romans. Their task was to survey their assigned chapter, choose one word or phrase, and define it. For example:

- Salvation
- Sanctification
- Sovereignty
- Flesh
- The law
- Election
- Faith
- Impute
- Judgment seat of Christ
- Justification
- Predestined
- Propitiation
- Reconciliation
- Righteousness
- Sin

The words were listed on the board, but there were only fifteen entries. Who did not report a word? More importantly, what chapter doesn't have a difficult word to add to the list? The one person who did not offer a word had Romans 16. When you read it, you will see why the student did not choose a word. The whole chapter is not a theological treatise but the end of a letter where Paul offers thanks, affirmation, and encouragement for specific people in the church. Knowing this brings up a few questions:

- Who are they?
- Why are they so important to Paul?
- Why is it important to you? Today?

Meet the first church of the Christian family who likely never met Jesus personally but who loved the Savior and served the community of faith:

- "I commend to you our sister Phoebe, a deacon of the church in Cenchreae. I ask you to receive her in the Lord in a way worthy of his people and to give her any help she may need from you, for she has been the benefactor of many people, including me" (Romans 16:1, 2).
- "Greet Priscilla and Aquila, my co-workers in Christ Jesus. They risked their lives for me. Not only I but all the churches of the Gentiles are grateful to them" (Romans 16:3, 4).
- "Greet my dear friend Epenetus, who was the first convert to Christ in the province of Asia" (Romans 16:5).
- "Greet Mary, who worked very hard for you" (Romans 16:6).
- "Greet Andronicus and Junia, my fellow Jews who have been in prison with me. They are outstanding among the apostles, and they were in Christ before I was" (Romans 16:7).
- "Greet Ampliatus, my dear friend in the Lord" (Romans 16:8).
- "Greet Urbanus, our co-worker in Christ, and my dear friend Stachys" (Romans 16:9).

Who are these people? They are believers who showed up to work hard, suffer with other believers, and risk their necks for the gospel. Paul personally knew everyone on this list. Are you curious about their stories? What did they risk for their faith? How did they know that God was calling them to serve? How do you share your love with your friends who are and are not believers?

Why are they important to you today? If the letter to the Romans were written today, would people like you, your friends, coworkers, and fellow followers of Christ be listed on the page instead of Phoebe, Andronicus, and Stachys? Words such as *sin*, *faith*, and *salvation* are only words until they are fleshed out in people's lives.

In the end, Paul offers a blessing that is also a prophecy about the church, saying: "The God of peace will soon crush Satan under your feet. The grace of our Lord Jesus be with you" (Romans 16:20).

With every kind word and every act of service, the work of God moves forward. May your every good work in the name of Christ be seasoned with grace.

INSIDE OUT

- In Romans 16, what specific observations can you make about the people mentioned?
- What specific observations can you make from these verses about Paul as a leader?
- What kind of qualities are affirmed and valued by Paul in the work of the gospel?
- Read the blessing in Romans 16:20. What would it look like today if you turned the blessing into a mission statement to follow?
- Consider the following texts:

    - But every spirit that does not acknowledge Jesus is not from God. This is the spirit of the antichrist, which you have heard is coming and even now is already in the world.

      You, dear children, are from God and have overcome them, because the one who is in you is greater than the one who is in the world (1 John 4:3, 4).

    - "See, it is I who created the blacksmith
who fans the coals into flame
and forges a weapon fit for its work.
And it is I who have created the destroyer to wreak havoc;
no weapon forged against you will prevail,
and you will refute every tongue that accuses you.
This is the heritage of the servants of the LORD,
and this is their vindication from me,"
declares the LORD (Isaiah 54:16, 17).

    - So he said to me, "This is the word of the LORD to Zerubbabel: 'Not by might nor by power, but by my Spirit,' says the LORD Almighty" (Zechariah 4:6).

    - The seventy-two returned with joy and said, "Lord, even the demons submit to us in your name."

      He replied, "I saw Satan fall like lightning from heaven. I have given you authority to trample on snakes and scorpions and to overcome all the power of the enemy; nothing will harm you. However, do not rejoice that the spirits submit to you, but rejoice that your names are written in heaven" (Luke 10:17–20).

51. THE GREAT ROOM

Day after day, in the temple courts and from house to house, they never stopped teaching and proclaiming the good news that Jesus is the Messiah.

—Acts 5:42

Small congregations have always been the makeup of God's ideal community called the church. Whether it's a couple studying in the garden or a family having evening worship—small groups are the church. One small church of thirty people chose this name and tagline for their gathering: "The Great Room—big enough for everyone but small enough to feel like home."

In the biblical account of Creation, God says: "*Let us* make mankind in our image, in our likeness" (Genesis 1:26; emphasis added). By nature, God is community. Humans are made in the image of God or to reflect God's likeness. In the very fabric of your being, there is the impulse to relate to others. If you long for a sense of "one another" and "each other," the obstacle will be the selfishness that finds a foothold in the human heart. So if we yearn for real community, why is it so difficult to attain? What keeps people from embracing the kind of relationships that they were wired for?

Since God made people with the notion of community in mind, humanity will always be more alive, more faithful, and more effective when they commune together under the banner of God's purpose.

During the Flood, the church consisted of only eight faithful people. It only took a church of three faithful young men to cause the kingdoms of the world to pay attention to the God of heaven (Daniel 3). The launch the "kingdom of God campaign" needed only a handful of women selfless enough to fund the project (Luke 8:1–3). Sometimes the church is simply four unnamed friends whose faith restores a friend (Mark 2:1–5), and other times it is a multitude of three thousand who experience the outpouring of the Holy Spirit (Acts 2).

It is natural to meet with others in community. In the times of the early church, the persecution drove believers from large gatherings to meeting in houses for community. The names and places you might recall from previous stories, but consider the house church in the Bible.

Perhaps if the Bible were written today, the names might be more familiar, but notice the church that Phoebe attends in Cenchreae (Romans 16:1, 2), or visit the assembly that meets at Gaius's house in Corinth (Romans 16:23, 24; 1 Corinthians 1:14).

Priscilla and Aquila had a solid group in their house (Romans 16:3–5; Acts 18:1–26; 1 Corinthians 16:19), as did Nympha in Laodicea (Colossians 4:15).

Lydia led a church that met outside in Philippi, and Philemon hosted a gathering in Colossae (Acts 16:9–15; Philemon 2)

Around the world, in every age, the assembly gathers. It's God's plan to convey His love to the world in twos, threes, tens, and more. In whatever shape, size, or style, the church is God's chosen method for reaching the world with His grace.

INSIDE OUT

- What is your sense of house churches? Are they a fad or the better option for people today?
- In what ways does your church function like a family?
- What are the limitations of small groups or house churches?
- Imagine if the following scenarios happened today. How do you see the human and the supernatural in the stories below?
  - On the first day of the week we came together to break bread. Paul spoke to the people and, because he intended to leave the next day, kept on talking until midnight. There were many lamps in the upstairs room where they were meeting. Seated in a window was a young man named Eutychus, who was sinking into a deep sleep as Paul talked on and on. When he was sound asleep, he fell to the ground from the third story and was picked up dead. Paul went down, threw himself on the young man and put his arms around him. "Don't be alarmed," he said. "He's alive!" Then he went upstairs again and broke bread and ate. After talking until daylight, he left. The people took the young man home alive and were greatly comforted (Acts 20:7–12).

  - A few days later, when Jesus again entered Capernaum, the people heard that he had come home. They gathered in such large numbers that there was no room left, not even outside the door, and he preached the word to them. Some men came, bringing to him a paralyzed man, carried by four of them. Since they could not get him to Jesus because of the crowd, they made an opening in the roof above Jesus by digging through it and then lowered the mat the man was lying on. When Jesus saw their faith, he said to the paralyzed man, "Son, your sins are forgiven."

Now some teachers of the law were sitting there, thinking to themselves, "Why does this fellow talk like that? He's blaspheming! Who can forgive sins but God alone?"

Immediately Jesus knew in his spirit that this was what they were thinking in their hearts, and he said to them, "Why are you thinking these things? Which is easier: to say to this paralyzed man, 'Your sins are forgiven,' or to say, 'Get up, take your mat and walk'? But I want you to know that the Son of Man has authority on earth to forgive sins." So he said to the man, "I tell you, get up, take your mat and go home." He got up, took his mat and walked out in full view of them all. This amazed everyone and they praised God, saying, "We have never seen anything like this" (Mark 2:1–12).

- The night before Herod was to bring him to trial, Peter was sleeping between two soldiers, bound with two chains, and sentries stood guard at the entrance. Suddenly an angel of the Lord appeared and a light shone in the cell. He struck Peter on the side and woke him up. "Quick, get up!" he said, and the chains fell off Peter's wrists.

  Then the angel said to him, "Put on your clothes and sandals." And Peter did so. "Wrap your cloak around you and follow me," the angel told him. Peter followed him out of the prison, but he had no idea that what the angel was doing was really happening; he thought he was seeing a vision. They passed the first and second guards and came to the iron gate leading to the city. It opened for them by itself, and they went through it. When they had walked the length of one street, suddenly the angel left him.

  Then Peter came to himself and said, "Now I know without a doubt that the Lord has sent his angel and rescued me from Herod's clutches and from everything the Jewish people were hoping would happen."

  When this had dawned on him, he went to the house of Mary the mother of John, also called Mark, where many people had gathered and were praying. Peter knocked at the outer entrance, and a servant named Rhoda came to answer the door. When she recognized Peter's voice, she was so overjoyed she ran back without opening it and exclaimed, "Peter is at the door!"

  "You're out of your mind," they told her. When she kept insisting that it was so, they said, "It must be his angel."

But Peter kept on knocking, and when they opened the door and saw him, they were astonished. Peter motioned with his hand for them to be quiet and described how the Lord had brought him out of prison. "Tell James and the other brothers and sisters about this," he said, and then he left for another place.

In the morning, there was no small commotion among the soldiers as to what had become of Peter. After Herod had a thorough search made for him and did not find him, he cross-examined the guards and ordered that they be executed (Acts 12:6–19).

52. GROW

Therefore, rid yourselves of all malice and all deceit, hypocrisy, envy, and slander of every kind. Like newborn babies, crave pure spiritual milk, so that by it you may grow up *in your salvation, now that you have tasted that the Lord is good.* As you come *to him, the living Stone—rejected by humans but chosen by God and precious to him—you also, like living stones, are being built into a spiritual house to be a holy priesthood, offering spiritual sacrifices acceptable to God through Jesus Christ.*

—1 Peter 2:1–5; emphasis added

Peter reminds his readers that "you also, like living stones, are being built into a spiritual house" (1 Peter 2:5). Consider a few starting points in Peter's observation about the faith community.

Avoid the things that entangle you. Even though it's not popular to address the problem, it is really the only place to begin. Jesus told the parable about seeds and soil, and the key part is the heart. When your heart is free, you are on fertile ground, and God's grace grows in you. When your heart has so much competition that the weeds flourish, even the strongest plant struggles. How? Hebrews speaks about how to disentangle your heart by focusing on the person of Christ, saying, "Therefore, since we are surrounded by such a great cloud of witnesses, let us throw off everything that hinders and the sin that so easily entangles. And let us run with perseverance the race marked out for us, fixing our eyes on Jesus, the pioneer and perfecter of faith. For the joy set before him he endured the cross, scorning its shame, and sat down at the right hand of the throne of

God" (Hebrews 12:1, 2). Saying, "Just focus on Jesus" is predictable, but as you wrestle with the process described in Hebrews, you will cultivate the habit.

Nourish and grow like children. Growth comes when you give God access to your heart by reading His Word personally and collectively, praying, serving, giving, worshiping, eating, and experiencing the joy of fellowship with others. As Paul admonishes, "So then, just as you received Christ Jesus as Lord, continue to live your lives in him rooted and built up in him, strengthened in the faith as you were taught, and overflowing with thankfulness" (Colossians 2:6, 7).

Know this: you will not grow alone in your walk. It requires personal sacrifices of time, energy, and sometimes money, but the work of growing up toward God is strengthening your relationships with others.

Consider one more starting point—show up. *Come to the place* where the community builds a household of faith.

Even if it is simply a small group of friends who share your desire for growth and mission, start by gathering. There are no easy steps or a perfect process; simply come together and start. The book of Acts contains story after story of people coming together—and the results are obvious. So when is the right time to start? "But encourage one another daily, as long as it is called 'Today,' so that none of you may be hardened by sin's deceitfulness" (Hebrews 3:13).

INSIDE OUT

- The maxim offered as a starting point for believers is: "Don't just go to church, be the church." If you were to start a brand-new church in your area, describe what that faith community would look like.
- What are the practices and characteristics you would hope for in a new church?
- What can you start doing today in your effort to be the church?
- Consider the following texts:

    - Just as a body, though one, has many parts, but all its many parts form one body, so it is with Christ. For we were all baptized by one Spirit so as to form one body—whether Jews or Gentiles, slave or free—and we were all given the one Spirit to drink. Even so the body is not made up of one part but of many (1 Corinthians 12:12–14).

    - "Again, truly I tell you that if two of you on earth agree about anything they ask for, it will be done for them by my Father in heaven. For where two or three gather in my name, *there am I with them*" (Matthew 18:19, 20; emphasis added).

- The God of peace will soon crush Satan under your feet. The grace of our Lord Jesus be with you (Romans 16:20).
- Then the dragon was enraged at the woman and went off to wage war against the rest of her offspring—those who keep God's commands and hold fast their testimony about Jesus (Revelation 12:17).